bathrooms

the *smart* approach to design

CREATIVE HOMEOWNER®

bathrooms

the *smart* approach to design

CREATIVE HOMEOWNER®, Upper Saddle River, New Jersey

CRE▲TIVE
HOMEOWNER®

A Division of Federal Marketing Corp.
Upper Saddle River, NJ

BATHROOMS: THE SMART APPROACH TO DESIGN

SENIOR EDITOR **Kathie Robitz**
PROOFREADER **Sara M. Markowitz**
PHOTO COORDINATOR AND
DIGITAL IMAGING SPECIALIST **Mary Dolan**
INDEXER **Schroeder Indexing Services**
SERIES DESIGN CONCEPT **Glee Barre, David Geer**
LAYOUT **David Geer**
FRONT COVER PHOTOGRAPHY **Eric Roth, design: aquidneckproperties.com**
BACK COVER PHOTOGRAPHY *top* **Eric Roth, design: morseconstructions.com;** *bottom* **Bob Greenspan, stylist: Susan Andrews**

CREATIVE HOMEOWNER

VICE PRESIDENT AND PUBLISHER **Timothy O. Bakke**
MANAGING EDITOR **Fran J. Donegan**
ART DIRECTOR **David Geer**
PRODUCTION COORDINATOR **Sara M. Markowitz**

Current Printing (last digit)
10 9 8 7 6 5 4 3 2 1

Manufactured in the United States of America

Bathrooms: The Smart Approach to Design
Library of Congress Control Number: 2009925793
ISBN-10: 1-58011-474-1
ISBN-13: 978-1-58011-474-5

CREATIVE HOMEOWNER®
A Division of Federal Marketing Corp.
24 Park Way
Upper Saddle River, NJ 07458
www.creativehomeowner.com

Planet Friendly Publishing
✓ Made in the United States
✓ Printed on Recycled Paper
Text: 10%   Cover: 10%
Learn more: www.greenedition.org
GREEN EDITION

acknowledgments

The editors wish to thank designers Helene Goodman, IIDA; Susan Obercian, of European Country Kitchens; and Lucianna Samu for their contributions to this book.

We would also like to acknowledge the helpful information provided by the National Kitchen and Bath Association.

contents

introduction

Every room in your home has the potential to showcase your personal style, and your bathroom is no exception. Nowadays, bathrooms combine function with style, incorporating materials, surfaces, and textures that used to be confined to other areas of the home. In addition, there are many functional elements that bathrooms contain, including fixtures, fittings, cabinets, lighting, and ventilation systems.

The many options in fixtures, materials, and finishes that are available today allow you to create your own style in the bath.

Bathrooms: The Smart Approach to Design will

- explain all of these components

- explain the features that will fit in best with your lifestyle and needs

- highlight stylish features you can make your own.

Want a modern sink, a Euro-style bathtub, or traditional fixtures? How about marble countertops, tile floors, or mirrored accents on the walls? Go for it—any style can be incorporated into your home to create a bathroom you will love for both the way it functions and its good looks.

Bathroom decor may run the gamut from ultra modern to classic, such Old World, above, or a combination of contemporary and nostalgic styles, right.

chapter 1
thinking ahead

t can be a good idea to remodel or add another bathroom, even in a tough economy. An updated design or a second bath will increase the value and livability of your house. The most important thing you can do prior to the start of your project is to prepare. Know what you need, what you'd love to have, and how you're going to pay for it. And find the best people to get the job done right. This is one of those remodeling projects that you'll never regret!

Thinking about adding a bath or remodeling an old one? Plan ahead to make the most of what you can afford to spend.

Plan to Save

Once you decide to remodel or add another bath to your house, you'll have to do some important research and planning. Becoming informed and knowing exactly what you want, how much you can or are willing to spend, and who is going to do the work will help you avoid some of the pitfalls that can cost you time and money.

Few people actually like to crunch numbers. However, establishing a budget is the only way to determine the size and scope of the project you can afford to design. It is disappointing to plan a luxurious bath, complete with spa features, only to find that you can barely afford a rain shower and a heated towel bar. Set priorities.

When you're looking at financing options, try to avoid paying cash. If it comes down to a choice between laying out cash for remodeling or for buying a new car, always go the cash route for the car and finance the remodeling. You can deduct the interest of the home-improvement loan from your taxes; you can't deduct the interest on a car loan. Unfortunately, many homeowners will gladly put money up front for a remodeling project and finance the car. It doesn't make sense.

It also doesn't make sense to set aside money or sign a loan for thousands of dollars without getting a handle on where that money is going. How much time would you spend investigating new cars before buying? You would probably read performance reports on various makes and models, then test drive several vehicles before finally making a purchase. Approach a home-improvement loan the same way. Take the time to investigate your financing options and all of the products and services for which you will be paying.

And don't forget: when seeking estimates, comparison shop for contractors. Use the plans and specifications for your new bathroom to get equivalent bids. If you can't draw them yourself, pay an architect or designer to do it.

get more information

@ www.NKBA.org
www.NARI.org

2 shop wisely

3 save water

the top 10
Planning Points

1 set realistic goals Make a list of must-haves; then add amenities you'd like to have—if the budget will allow.

2 research products Look for the best you can afford. Compare prices and features.

9 personal preferences

3 check out "green" alternatives Incorporate some earth-friendly products, such as water-conserving fixtures, into your bath design.

4 interview several contractors Check their references and the contractors' standing with the Better Business Bureau.

5 get it in writing Among other things:
- the payment schedule
- specifics of the job
- a start date and a reasonable timetable for completion

6 expect the unexpected Build a cushion into your budget.

7 make arrangements Keep in mind that you may have to stay elsewhere for a few days at some point during the project—especially if it's the only bathroom in the house.

8 obtain permits This is a rule not to be broken. Never let anyone tell you to skip this step. Permits and building codes exist for a reason—your safety. Ignoring them may cost you not only financially but personally, as well.

9 consider your habits and lifestyle A gorgeous jetted tub may be some people's idea of luxe bathing. But if you are strictly a shower person, don't be afraid to forgo the tub and build a fabulous shower in its place.

10 waste not If you are thinking green when shopping for new products and materials for your bath, go a step further and consider what you have that you can reuse or repurpose.

Help!

Ask friends and neighbors to recommend professionals in your area. You can also check online or in the local paper. Whenever you hire people to work in your home, first take the time to research them carefully. Your home is likely your largest single asset. Don't take chances with it unnecessarily. Interview professionals, and follow up on their references. Ask tough questions. Call state agencies and trade associations to check credentials, and always work with licensed contractors.

Whomever you choose to help remodel the bath will end up knowing you and your family better than your lawyer or doctor. He or she will see you first thing in the morning and after a hard day at the office. That person will be a part of your family for the length of time it takes to complete the project. Check out all professionals as closely as you would a tenant.

Also remember, the people you hire to work on the

project are in your home. You have every right to tell them not to smoke, play music, curse, or eat inside. You can even tell them how and where to store tools and materials around your home. Be reasonable, but make a set of rules before work begins, and ask your contractor to enforce them. You could include this in your contract, which gives you legal grounds for making your demands. However, in most cases, a reputable contractor will make sure that workers are respectful of your wishes.

The master bath pictured here and on the opposite page caters to both the aesthetic and the functional requirements of its owners, thanks to careful planning. The owners found design and building professionals who understood their needs and with whom they could communicate.

STEP 1 architects

If you're planning a significant structural change, such as expanding space or your bath will be part of a larger remodeling project, consulting an architect is a wise move. Among other things, an architect will be sensitive to making sure that the new bath blends with your home's original architecture. Be sure to find one who specializes in residential design. Look for the letters "AIA" after an architect's name. This indicates his or her membership in the American Institute of Architects, a national organization of licensed professionals. For a referral to an architect in your area, go to www.AIA.org.

STEP 2 CBDs

Certified Bath Designers, or CBDs, are trained professionals who are certified specifically in bath design and remodeling by the National Kitchen and Bath Association (NKBA). Because CBDs are specialists, they can advise you with regard to spatial issues and floor plans, as well as offer you advice about the latest trends and innovations in bath products that would suit your needs and lifestyle. Check local bath-design showrooms or home centers to find a qualified professional—with the letters "CBD" after his or her name. Or, log on to www.NKBA.org for a referral.

STEP 3 interior designers

Interior designers do not make structural changes but work with color, pattern, texture, and furnishings to shape a design. He or she will collaborate with an architect or other remodeling professional to create an overall look for your bath. You may want to contact an interior designer if you are making significant cosmetic changes. The letters "ASID" after an interior designer's name indicate membership in the American Society of Interior Designers, a national organization of qualified licensed professionals. Your local or state chapter can refer you to an ASID member in your area.

STEP 4 contractors

A contractor is a good choice if you have already hired an architect to design the bathroom or if you are not making substantial structural changes to the room. One good example of when to choose a remodeling contractor is when you are simply upgrading fixtures or reconfiguring the existing space for a better arrangement.

■ **Design-build remodeling firms** offer one-stop shopping for design services and construction provided by designers and remodelers who are on staff. If something goes wrong, you only have to make one call. There's no buck-passing here.

A spacious floor plan that accommodates a double vanity, a large walk-in shower, and a separate soaking tub may require additional space. Expanding an existing home is a large and costly project. Most people will obtain a home-improvement loan to get the job done. Interest on such loans is usually tax deductible, but consult your accountant.

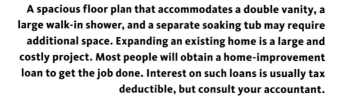

Financing

Any bank or lending institution will tell you how much you can afford to spend on your home-remodeling project. But if you feel more comfortable running a test on your own, here is a quick and simple overview of how banks figure out what you can spend.

The debt-to-income (DTI) ratio

This tells a lender if you can handle more debt on your current level of income. While each lender has its own approved DTI ratio, the average is normally at least 45 percent.

Current monthly expenses	$_____
Add the estimated monthly remodeling payment	+_____
Total expenses	$_____
Divide by your gross monthly income	÷_____
This is your DTI ratio	_____%

How to find your maximum payment for remodeling

If your DTI doesn't qualify for financing options, you may need to lower the monthly remodeling expenditure. This calculation will show you how low you need to go.

Gross monthly income	$_____
Multiply by lender's DTI ratio	x_____
Subtotal	$_____
Subtract your total monthly expenses (minus the estimated remodeling payment)	−_____
This gives you your maximum payment of	$_____

If the last line is negative, you may have to scale back your plans or do the work yourself on a very tight budget. A negative number means that you won't be receiving funds from a lender. However, you can check out other funding options. For example, a consolidation loan will allow you to incorporate your current debts into your home-improvement loan. Firstly, this will lower the monthly cost of your current debts. Secondly, this loan allows you to deduct the interest from your taxes, something that you can't do on other forms of debt.

If your credit score is good, you can find a variety of other forms of financing as well. You could take out a loan against investments, borrow against your credit card, or the perennial favorite: obtain a private loan from a family member.

Q&A

Can you get out of a contract? What happens if something unforseen happens that may affect going through with the project?

what the experts say

There is a grace period wherein you have the legal right to change your mind. This is called the "Right of Rescission." You can do this within three days of signing the contract without any liability if the contract was obtained at any place other than the designer's or contractor's office—your home, for instance. Federal law mandates that consumers must be made aware of this right in writing. Ask your contractor before you sign anything.

what real people do

Frank and Betty were excited about adding a master bath to their 50-year-old house, but life happens. Just one week after signing a contract with a home-improvement company, Frank had a health crisis that meant months of recuperation at home and additional strains on the couple's budget. Several days past the grace period, their legal right to cancel the job had expired—or did it?

Actually, Frank and Betty had never been properly informed of their right. The contractor failed to include it in the contract. By law, the Right of Rescission remains open beyond three days (up to three years) if the notice is not given or, as in Frank and Betty's case, is not provided in the required manner.

To ensure that you get what you want, put it in writing. If you like sleek, compact fixtures, such as the toilet and lav above, specify the make and model numbers. Unless an item is custom, such as the vanity below, provide manufacturer names, sizes, and colors in the contract.

The Write Stuff

You have a right to a specific and binding contract. The more specific details it contains, the better. The details will save you in the long run. Remember: anytime you enter into an agreement, you are venturing into the legal world of a litigious society. So get everything in writing, but know what you're signing—and never sign an incomplete contract.

For starters:

■ Make sure the contract contains the contractor's name and proper business name as it appears on the business license, as well as the company's address, phone number, and business license number.

■ Details of everything the contractor will do, including such things as daily and final cleanup and security measures

■ A complete list of materials and products, including size, color, model, and brand name of each one

■ The approximate start and completion dates

do this... not that

accepting deliveries

Let your contractor sign for deliveries unless you personally ordered the materials or are prepared to be liable for them. Signing for materials is your contractor's responsibility. Imagine what would happen if you signed for the wrong floor tiles. You would be responsible. Don't take chances. Let your contractor shoulder the burden of tracking down incomplete, incorrect, or damaged orders.

Special orders, such as this tub, can be tricky, and it's not uncommon for the wrong model to be delivered. Leave it to your contractor to handle these things.

What Else?

To prevent changes being made without your knowledge, your signature should be required on all plans before work begins. If you want to make a change during the course of the project, you'll probably need what is called a "change order." The procedure for handling changes should be spelled out in your contract and should require both your signature and the contractor's.

You can also ask for a listing and full description of warranties that cover materials and workmanship. Warranties are normally in force for one year and should be identified as either "full" or "limited."

Finally, it's wise to ask your contractor for waivers of lien, which release you from liabilities for subcontractors and manufacturers. At the end of the job, ask for a final lien waiver for each person who worked on the project to protect yourself from third-party debts and obligations. You don't want to be forced, legally, into paying for the job a second time because the contractor never made good on his debts.

All of the above should be part of the contract, along with anything else you feel should be spelled out clearly and in writing.

Don't make changes if you don't have to, because they create additional work and delay progress. For example, substituting a wall-mounted faucet, right, for one installed on the deck of a lav or vanity would entail opening and retiling a portion of the wall.

Insurance and Permits

All contractors should have current liability insurance and worker's compensation to cover employees while they are working on your property. If you are still worried about your legal liabilities should an injury occur while someone is working on your property, talk to your insurance carrier and attorney. You may want your insurance agent to review the plans for the new bathroom and adjust your homeowner's coverage during the length of the project.

Never allow work to be done on your home without a legal permit. Permits may require fees and inspections—two things everyone would like to avoid—but they ensure the project conforms to the latest building codes.

A bathroom remodel requires hiring various workers. Tiling and plumbing, left, call for different skills than installing paneling on a wall, opposite. Your contractor will hire qualified people and should be responsible for their on-the-job safety.

do this... not that

wait a minute, there...

What if your contractor substitutes another product for the one specified in your written agreement? That is not cool, and you do not have to accept it. Tell him or her that you will only allow changes that have been properly outlined in writing and have both of your signatures. Any change order should include a detailed description of the work that will be involved and an estimate of the time and cost of making the change.

A bath can be your personal spa—but not if your contractor ignores your stated preferences.

Check, Please

Don't hesitate to ask about any detail concerning the project. It's your house, and it's your money. The more information you have, the happier you will be with the result. This is particularly true when selecting products or figuring out warranty coverage. Find out what is and isn't covered by warranties. Many manufacturers won't honor a warranty if an amateur fix-it job has been attempted. Avoid disasters by calling your contractor or the manufacturer for guidance about repairs.

Which brings us to: should you do any of the job yourself? That depends on two things—your skills and whether or not a licensed professional is required by law. Take the quiz on the opposite page to see whether you've got what it takes; regarding the latter, check with your building department.

If you want to get hands-on, consider taking a class at your local home-improvement center. You could learn how to tile a new countertop for your vanity or replace an old faucet. Find out when the next class will be held. The bonus? It's free.

Should You Do It Yourself?

Before you make the decision to tackle a bath remodeling project on your own, take a few minutes to answer the following questions. This exercise will help you determine whether or not you have the necessary skills and abilities. Be honest with yourself.

Yes   No   Do you enjoy physical work?

Yes   No   Are you persistent and patient? (Do you have reliable work habits? Once the project is started, will it get finished?)

Yes   No   Do you have all the tools needed and, more importantly, the skills required to do the job?

Yes   No   Are your skills at the level of quality you need for this project?

Yes   No   Do you have time to complete the project? (Always double or triple the time estimated for a DIY project, unless you are highly skilled and familiar with that type of project.)

Yes   No   Will it matter if the project remains unfinished for a period of time?

Yes   No   Are you prepared to handle the kind of stress this project will create in your family relationships?

Yes   No   Have you done all of the steps involved in the project before?

Yes   No   Have you obtained the installation instructions from the manufacturers of the various products and fixtures to determine whether this is a project you still want to undertake? (You can obtain them from most manufacturers before purchase to determine the steps involved in installation and the skill level required.)

Yes   No   Is this a job that you can accomplish completely by yourself, or will you need assistance? If you'll need help, what skill level is involved for your assistant? If you need a professional sub-contractor, do you have access to a skilled labor pool?

Yes   No   Are you familiar with local building codes and permit requirements? (Check into these matters before beginning work on your bathroom project.)

Yes   No   What will you do if something goes wrong and you can't handle it? (Most contractors are wary about taking on a botched DIY job, and many just won't. The liability is too high.)

Yes   No   Is it safe for you to do this project? (If you are unfamiliar with roofing [for a bathroom addition] or do not have fall-protection restraints, you may not want to venture a roofing job. Similarly, if you know nothing about electricity, leave it to the professionals. Some jobs can have serious consequences if not performed correctly. Your health and safety should be the primary concerns.)

Yes   No   Can you obtain the materials you need? (Who will be your supplier?)

Yes   No   Are you attempting to do it yourself for financial reasons? (If so, have you looked at all your costs, including the cost of materials, your time, and the tools you need to purchase? If you are new to the DIY game, you may also want to consider the cost to correct any mistakes you may make. Will it still be a cost-saving venture given all of these factors?)

Yes   No   If you are trying DIY for your personal satisfaction, can you really guarantee a job that will be well done? (If it doesn't come out right, how will you feel? Will you need the money to redo any unsatisfactory work? Will you have it? Will you be able to live with mistakes?)

The simplicity of its style belies the exacting execution of all of the features that make this master bath so perfectly pampering. **Far right:** A frameless glass shower enclosure keeps the elegant Carrara marble subway tiles on view. A rainshower and a hand-held sprayer offer versatility. For more indulgence, there is a large soaking tub in the room as well. **Top right:** A heated towel rack is conveniently located on the wall above the tub. The location of

it's in the details *

the property allows the windows to remain uncovered. **Right:** The room also features a pair of vanities. Although only one is pictured here, they are identical.

see more Carrara tile
www.carraratiles.com
www.annsacks.com

thinking ahead

Abundant natural light and natural materials emphasize this bathroom's earth-friendly point of view. **Far right:** Because bathrooms are typically big water guzzlers, the homeowner and designer looked for water-efficient fixtures. In addition, the wall-mounted lav and toilet are ADA compliant, which means they conform to the standards outlined in the Americans with Disabilities Act.

Top right: In one corner, a modest-size shower takes in sunlight thanks to the

it's in the
details ✳

glass enclosure, which is partially frosted for privacy. **Right:** The deep tub has the added convenience of a hand-held sprayer for rinsing hair or bathing the family pet.

size up your space

How you arrange space will be an important part of your new bathroom. Although it's not the largest room in the house, and certainly one where you won't be spending a lot of time, it can be efficient. Who will use it? Is it a master bath just for you, or will the entire family use this room? What kinds of features have to be incorporated into the design to make it work for your preferences? How large is the actual space? Here's how to work it out.

Think of your bathroom in terms of function. You can make any size room more efficient if you organize the physical space logically.

Assessing Your Needs

At the outset, make a list of what you would like your new bathroom to be and how you need it to function. Will it be your at-home spa? A shared bath for the family? Simply a practical extra bath? The type of bathroom—and who will use it—may determine its size and will certainly affect the products you select to finish it.

If you're remodeling an existing bath, it's good to make a list of what you don't like about it and what you hope to change. Is there enough storage? Is the lighting around the vanity or lav suitable for grooming? Are the fixtures functioning efficiently? Is the ventilation adequate?

Maybe you'd like to replace your one-piece tub and shower with an extra-deep soaker and a walk-in rain shower. Perhaps the materials—tiles, vanity countertop, faucets, light fixtures, and so forth—should be updated.

Take safety measures into account in your analysis. Are there enough ground-fault circuit interrupters (GFCIs)? These receptacles should be installed in wet areas, such as bathrooms, because they can sense an imbalance in the electrical circuit and cut the current in a fraction of a second. Unlike GFCIs, ordinary receptacles cannot protect you against the full force of an electrical shock.

Other safety concerns about an older bath can be the condition of the floor tiles—are they cracked or slippery? How old are the faucets? Are they equipped with antiscalding mechanisms?

Don't forget to take ergonomics into account, especially if older family members will use the room. Are the valves easy to open and close? Is it easy or difficult to enter the tub or shower? Are there grab bars?

Creative design can make a modest-size bath perform as though it is much larger. On one end of the layout, left, a half-wall and glass partition section off the bath and shower while admitting natural light into the entire room. Above, a pocket door closes off the water closet and takes up no floor space. There's plenty of room for grooming and adequate storage at the double vanity, opposite.

Can I replace a bathtub and small shower in my master bath with just a large walk-in shower? I heard that this was a no-no.

what the experts say

Real estate and remodeling experts both say that a house without a bathtub will lower the resale value. Most people with young children who are buying a house want at least one bathtub. However, you're talking about the master bath, and assuming there is another bathroom with a tub in your house, you're probably safe with just a shower, especially if it's large and has desirable spa features.

what real people do

Many people are forgoing a bathtub to make space for a large walk-in shower, especially when they are planning to stay in their house for at least five years. All the experts would agree that, in this case, the most important thing you can do is make your bath what you want it to be. For people who rarely, if ever, use the tub, a great shower makes a lot of sense.

In fact, when you put your house on the market, depending on who is buying, a glamorous custom shower for two with multiple showerheads and sprayers, steam, and other luxe features may even seal the deal.

Making a (Wish) List and Checking It Twice

Go ahead and make your wish list as long as you like. Remember: you're only wishing at this stage, so the sky's the limit. This is a good time to visit bath design showrooms and home centers and to jot down ideas that you may have seen in magazines or on TV. When it's available, note the cost. Go over your list, making sure that what you've got on it is both practical and affordable for your circumstances.

When you come up with a close-to-perfect plan, look for areas to trim expenses if you're going over budget. Decide what you really can't live without. If you still need to lower costs, where can you substitute or make compromises? For example, rather than selecting real stone, choose a ceramic field tile that looks like stone but is more affordable. Save the splurge on stone for accent areas, which require much fewer pieces and cost much less.

Look for bargains. Spend time browsing the Web, where you can comparison-shop and perhaps get a better deal on certain items.

Reserving tile for wet areas, such as a shower, opposite, can keep costs down. Natural materials and a connection with the outdoors, below left, are desirable, but they may come at a cost. For some, a large spa tub, below, is at the top of the wish list.

Layouts

Whether it's a full-size bath or a powder room, the arrangement of space plays a large role in how well the room will function. A bathroom addition to an outside wall of the house offers the best possibilities for unencumbered floor space. However, it will be the costliest. One way to save money is to bump out the wall by a few feet and extend the existing floor structure out over the foundation. Consult an architect or builder first, to make sure the structure is sound and can carry the additional load. Always inquire about local zoning ordinances and setback requirements that may affect your plans before proceeding. If you violate codes, you could be forced to remove the new construction.

If you can't improve the layout of an existing bath by building an addition, take a good look at areas that are next to the room, such as hallways or unused space under a stairway. Sometimes even a small amount of space stolen from a closet or an adjacent room can be the answer to your problem. If your family requires two bathrooms but there's only enough room for one, forego a spacious master bath for two smaller, side-by-side bathrooms. You'll save money this way, too, because the plumbing lines for both rooms will be right there.

Take a look at the layouts and arrangements on the opposite page and later in this chapter. Then start thinking about what might work best for you.

get more tile ideas

www.artistictile.com
www.ctioa.org

A custom tile design unites the separate areas of this master bath. The adjacent shower room, opposite, is harmonious with the tub, right, located in the main part of the bath. Investigate all the configurations that might suit your space and preferences.

Floor-Plan Ideas

Bathroom layouts are as varied today as those of kitchens. Here are a few floor plans you might consider for your project.

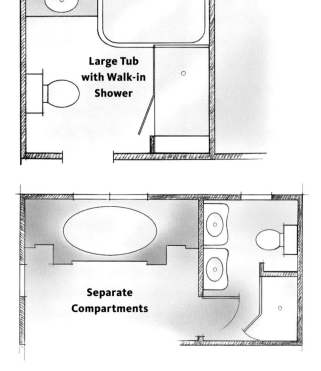

Large Tub with Walk-in Shower

Corner Shower

Separate Compartments

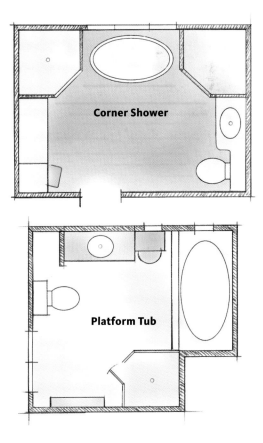

Platform Tub

STEP 1 measure and sketch

Start by taking measurements, beginning with the length and width of the room. Then working from one corner, measure the location of all windows, doors, and walls. Record the swing of each door.

Draw a rough sketch of the space. Measure and draw the cabinetry and plumbing fixtures, and indicate their heights. Measure the centerline of sinks, toilets, and bidets, and show how far the center of each of these fixtures is from the wall. Be sure to list the overall lengths and widths.

■ **Indicate light fixtures, outlets, and heat registers.** (See the sketch, below.) Note load-bearing walls.

■ **Make notations.** Indicate desired changes.

STEP 2 draw a floor plan

Transfer your drawing and notes to graph paper with grids marked at ¼-inch intervals. This formal drawing is called a "base map" or a "base plan." Draw it to a scale of ½ inch equal to 1 foot.

Refer to the base plan and your notes when you're creating a new layout for the space, which you will draw in the same manner.

When you are indicating new fixtures, be sure to adhere to the required front and side clearances. Keep in mind that state and local codes may apply. Ask about clearances when you apply for a permit if you are doing the actual work yourself. Of course, you can play it safe and consult a professional.

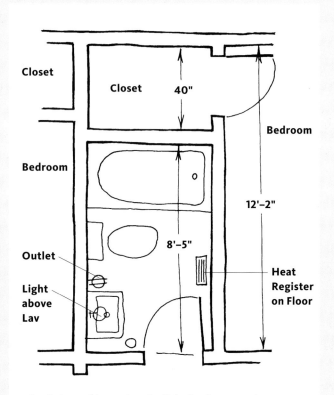

Begin by making a sketch of the bathroom as it now exists. Include any adjacent areas that might be used for expansion. Indicate fixtures and electrical and heating features.

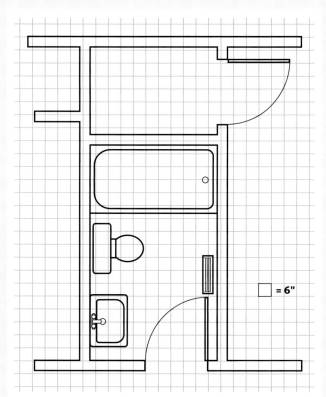

Use your rough sketch to create a base plan that is drawn to a scale of ½ inch to 1 foot. This time, be as accurate as possible when indicating measurements.

If floor space is limited, choose fixtures that are stylish but suit the scale of the room.

2 showers for two

5 half walls

the top 10
Best Uses of Space

1 water closets Many homeowners ask for a closed-door compartment, within the room, just for the toilet.

2 showers for two Even if you shower alone, it's great to have the space. Install multiple options for water-delivery.

7 wall fixtures

8 built-in storage

3 **a separate bathtub** If you've got room for it, keep the tub separate from the shower.

4 **double sinks and vanities** Not only does this arrangement allow two people to groom at the same time, it provides storage. If you don't have the space, see whether your layout can accommodate a pair of pedestal sinks.

5 **half walls** This is one way to create separate areas in a modest-size bathroom without closing off natural light coming from an outside wall.

6 **skylights and roof windows** Installing one of these units allows you to add natural light where adding a standard window is not possible.

7 **off the floor** Tight on floor space? Install a wall-mounted vanity, lav, or toilet. Faucets installed on the wall rather than on the lav deck or counter leave more space for your hair dryer and grooming products.

8 **built-in storage** Use space inside the wall between the studs to create open or closed storage.

9 **pocket doors** You gotta love 'em. These space-saving doors slide inside the wall rather than opening into the room.

10 **corner fixtures** Prefabricated showers, lavs, vanities, and toilets designed to tuck neatly into a corner are great solutions for small bath- or powder rooms.

Designing a Master Bath

Compartmentalizing space makes sense when a bath is shared. Some of the best floor plans for today's adult baths include a compartment just for the toilet (water closet) and separate bathing and showering, and grooming areas for two. This concept makes lots of sense, providing privacy and enough space for two people to comfortably use the bathroom at the same time. If your space cannot accommodate separate compartments, you could add half walls or partitions, which can divide space effectively—even in the smallest rooms.

Spa features are high on the list for most master bathroom remodelers, and they may include such amenities as a jetted or an extra-deep soaking tub, and spacious walk-in shower equipped with steam, massaging water jets, and stationary showerheads as well as handheld sprayers. Additional options to enhance bathing include chroma- and aromatherapy systems.

For homeowners who want spalike pampering, there is something quite luxurious about a walk-in shower bathed with natural light. Operable skylights (roof windows) in the showers, below left and opposite, also provide excellent ventilation.

Don't forget to include storage space for linens and grooming and cleaning products. As part of a large master suite, the bathroom may also connect to a walk-in closet or dressing area.

Other popular amenities for your consideration? A heated floor, TV, sound system, fireplace, gym, and access to an outdoor area. You are only limited by size and imagination—and some local codes. So go ahead, pamper yourself.

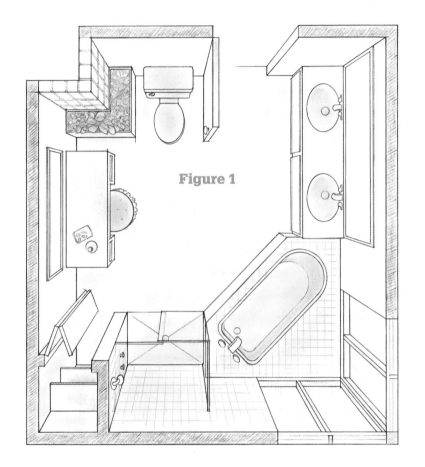

Figure 1

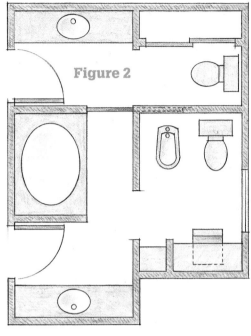

Figure 2

Figure One: An angled bathtub conserves floor space and allows for a double vanity.

Figure Two: An adjacent half-bath boosts a master bath's use.

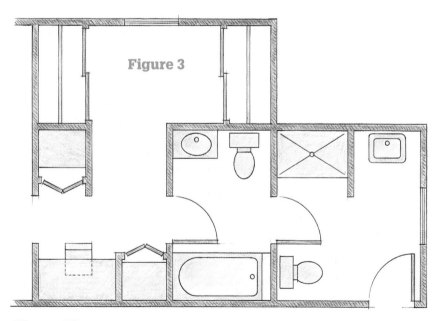

Figure 3

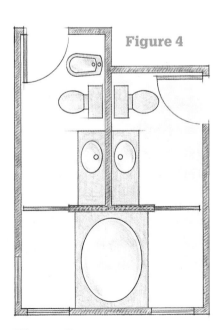

Figure 4

Figure Three: A grand layout provides two separate but connected bathrooms within a large master suite.

Figure Four: His and her zones open via pocket doors to a shared tub.

Side by side but separate, a large tub and shower occupy one end of a large master bathroom, above. This compact arrangement leaves space for a long double vanity and large mirror, below right. To keep the countertop uncluttered, the lav faucets have been wall mounted, below.

49

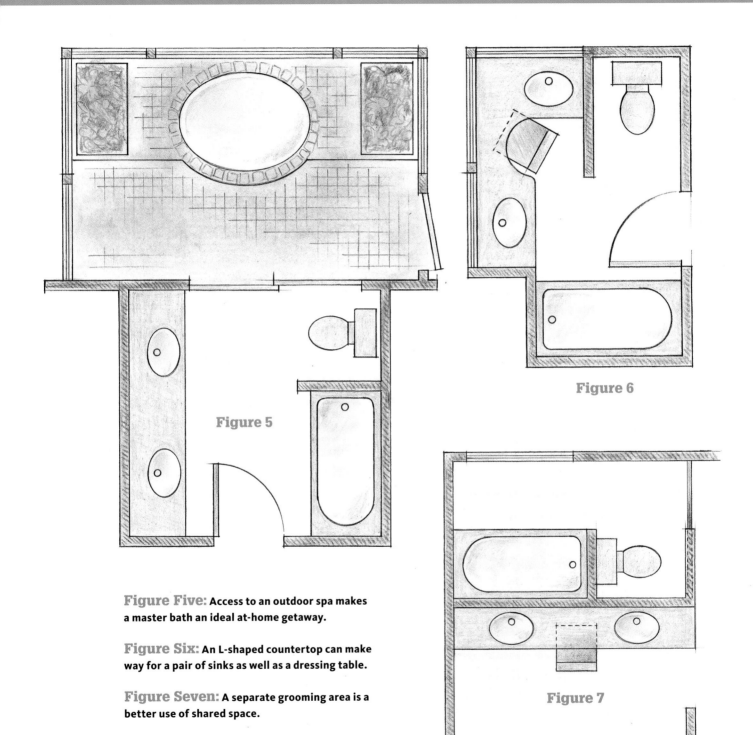

Figure 5

Figure 6

Figure 7

Figure Five: Access to an outdoor spa makes a master bath an ideal at-home getaway.

Figure Six: An L-shaped countertop can make way for a pair of sinks as well as a dressing table.

Figure Seven: A separate grooming area is a better use of shared space.

In a long and somewhat narrow room, the designer was able to keep the tub and shower next to each other (and avoid a longer plumbing line) by bumping the tub further into the room, above. His and her vanities, right and below, line up against one wall.

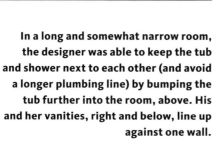

For this homeowner, there's nothing like nature for regaining calm and soothing the soul. **Far right:** Thanks to the secluded location of her home, she can unwind everyday in a warm bath overlooking a view of the hills beyond. When the morning sun is too bright, she adjusts the shades, lowering them to filter the light.

Top right: A built-in dresser makes practical use of a small nook at one end of the room. It sits next

it's in the details *

to the walk-in shower that features more pampering extras.
Right: Case in point is the use of water tiles, which are strategically located on the shower wall and can be aimed at any tired muscle.

Planning Shared Space

When families share a bath, creating an organized plan that serves all members of the household is important, especially when there are kids and older adults involved. If you can divide the space into distinct grooming, bathing, and toileting areas, you'll alleviate some of the issues that come up under this circumstance. If at all possible, provide storage for everyone's things. Choose a design that is easy to keep clean, fixtures that are comfortable for all, and faucets and hardware that are easy to operate. This isn't the place for getting too fancy, but you can be practical and stylish.

Clean lines and light colors help to keep small or shared bathrooms attractive and calming.

Family Bath Design Options

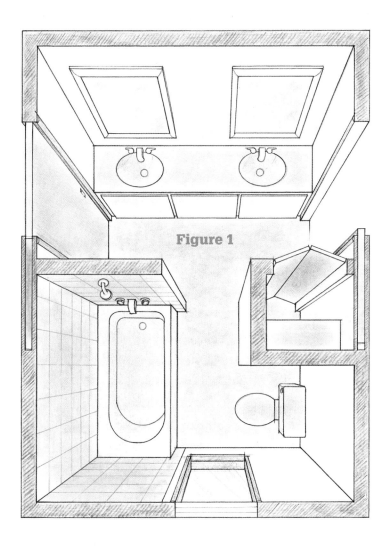

Figure 1

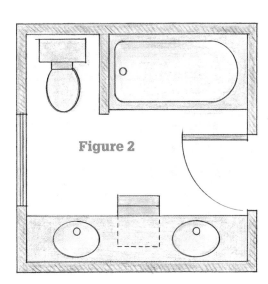

Figure 2

Figure One: Pocket doors, installed around this room, do not use up floor space, allowing for an improved floor plan.

Figure Two: A partition next to the toilet expands the use of a bathroom without a costly addition.

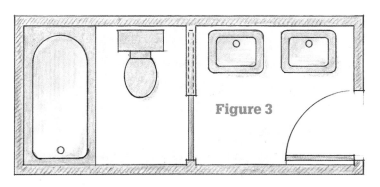

Figure 3

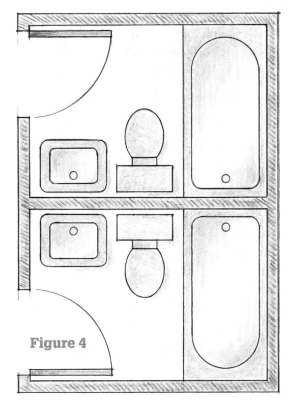

Figure 4

Figure Three: Locating the sinks, which are the most-used fixtures, nearest the door is logical.

Figure Four: Back-to-back plumbing creates two smaller bathrooms from one formerly large space.

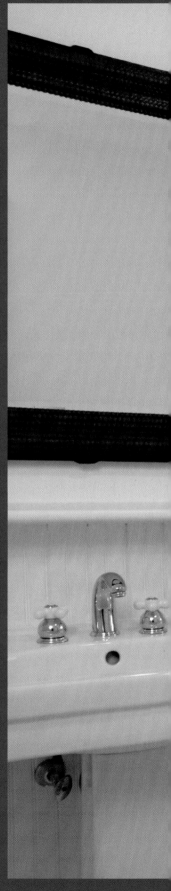

W hile retaining the spirit of the Lake Placid, N.Y., location, these homeowners created a master bath that is built for relaxing after a day on the water or on the slopes. A large jetted tub is the focal point of the room, which is on the second floor of the house and affords a pleasant view of the treetops.

Far right and right: Unassuming materials, such as the bead-board paneling and nostalgic faucet valves bring charm into the space. The owners used antique

it's in the
details ✱

frames to trim the mirrors over a pair of pedestal sinks. **Top right:** Side sconces reduce facial shadows.

find paneling
@ www.certainteed.com
www.beadboard.com

Partial Baths

Technically speaking, a bath with a shower but no tub is called a "three-quarter bath." Some homeowners choose this over a full bath with a combined tub and shower, especially when it gives them room for a spacious walk-in compartment with fancy amenities, such as steam and water jets, rain showers, or water tiles. And a glass enclosure can even make a small space feel larger.

Half baths, or powder rooms, can be a convenience on a floor without a full bath. Sometimes it's a strictly utilitarian facility, or it can be an elegant little jewel box dressed to the nines for company. Powder rooms require little space; you can even tuck one under the stairs. You can find small-scale fixtures, but always check codes for clearances.

It might be short on square footage, but this three-quarter layout is big on function. There's room for two at the vanity, below left, thanks to a pair of lavs that are small but do the job. At the other end, a walk-in shower, below, is plenty roomy. Glass comes to the rescue, again, keeping the look open and light.

Half- and Three-Quarter Baths

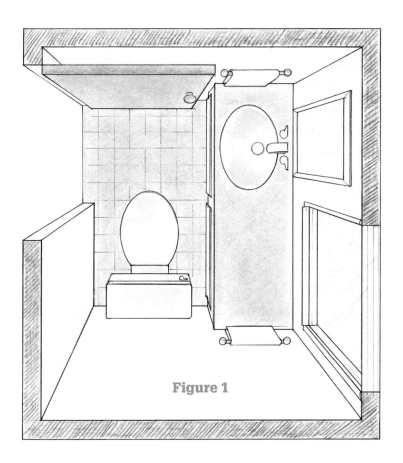

Figure 1

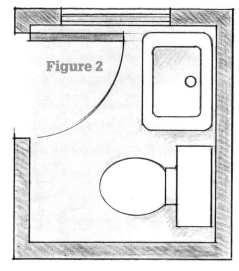

Figure 2

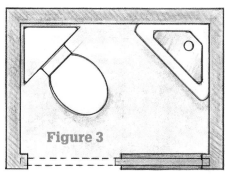

Figure 3

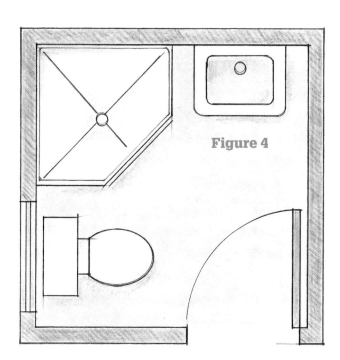

Figure 4

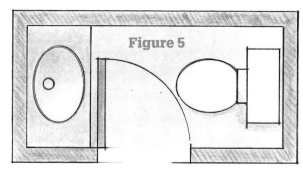

Figure 5

Figure One: A large vanity is helpful if a half-bath doubles as an extra grooming area on busy mornings.

Figure Two: Locate the sink and the toilet on the same wall to conserve floor space.

Figure Three: Corner fixtures and a pocket door are small-space solutions.

Figure Four: A corner shower unit can convert a half-bath into a three-quarter bath.

Figure Five: In a long, narrow room, place the toilet and the sink on opposite walls.

3 use corners

5 nip and tuck

the top 10
Half-Bath Tips

1 color Even if you feel timid about using deep colors elsewhere, go for it here. Kick it up a notch with
- a glossy finish
- texture

2 pattern Bold pattern in a tiny room? Absolutely! Use oversize wallpaper and fabric patterns. Large prints make big statements, and your powder room will look grand.

3 use corners and angles Angle a vanity in a corner. Install corner fixtures.

4 round it out Curved or round furnishings take the boxy look out of a small space.

5 nip and tuck Extend a portion of the vanity counter over a toilet tank.

8 go for glamour

4 round it out

10 special touches

6 install a pedestal sink A pedestal sink is pretty, and it makes good use of small space.

7 include good lighting It's important to install proper lighting in every bathroom. Remember, your guests may be using the powder room to touch up makeup.

8 go for glamour Splurge on special fixtures: a small chandelier, a handpainted lav, or gorgeous fittings.

9 use an antique Swap a standard vanity and retrofit an antique table, cabinet, or chest with a lav and faucet. This is a great way to create a

unique style statement—and you can sometimes find a bargain piece at a flea market or garage sale.

10 pamper your guests Include special hand towels, soaps, and lotions. Fresh flowers are always a beautiful touch.

Designed for Kids

A bathroom planned for the kids depends on their ages. Safety is always a concern, so install countertops or sinks that suit the height of the children who will be using the room if you can. If you don't want to have to replace these items as children grow, build a step into the vanity's toe-kick area.

Keep scale in mind when you're installing plumbing. In the shower, a handheld sprayer that a child can easily reach is a good idea. Lever-style valves are easier to operate than knobs or handles that are too large or uncomfortable for small hands. Most localities require installing faucets with antiscald devices. Use them, and make sure the water temperature is set at a level that won't scald tender skin.

If kids will share a bathroom, try at least to separate the toilet area. A pocket door can be a solution when you want to close off a small space because the door slides into the wall between the studs, not into the room.

Scaled down fixtures, left, make it easy for kids to wash up. A small handheld sprayer is easy for them to operate and is located at a suitable height on the shower wall, above. Sometimes a small stool is just the boost a child needs, opposite.

chapter 3
outfitting your bath

The fixtures you choose for your new bathroom will say as much about your commitment to the planet as they will about your style. You could seek the advice of a qualified designer to help with your choices, but chances are, you'll be doing a lot of the shopping on your own. So here's what today's market has to offer in terms of looks and engineering. Oh, but let's not forget the glamour factor—there are plenty of luxury features you may find too tempting to ignore.

Choosing fixtures isn't as simple as it was when you only had a few choices. But today's offerings let you create a custom bathing experience.

I'm ready to choose fixtures for my new bathroom, but I don't know where to begin. What will look right in my space?

what the experts say

Interior designer Helene Goodman, IIDA, says "Consider the style and setting of your home. If it's contemporary, for instance, choose fixtures that complement that style." Geometric shapes, hard angles, and clean lines are hallmarks of this look, while embellishments such as fluting and other classical details are more traditional. "Getting advice from a qualified interior designer could save you a costly mistake and time."

what real people do

"Typically, homeowners are willing to spend more on a master bathroom because this space will receive the most use on a daily basis," says Goodman. But the powder room is always a good place to do something a little different. It is not necessary to match the color of the sink to that of the toilet. Many of her clients, for example, choose a powder-room sink made of glass, metal, or stone.

Sometimes just choosing the right fittings can establish a look. Case in point: Jack and Elaine bought their new house because it was "move-in ready," they said. The master bath was "suped up and ultra-modern," but it seemed too "industrial-looking and cold" for their traditional taste. Rather than ripping out all of the fixtures, they swapped the polished chrome fittings for ones with an oil-rubbed bronze finish. Voilà! Instant warmth.

Today's Fixtures

Thanks partly to a dizzying array of glittering fixtures and fittings, today's bathroom can be described as beautiful, luxurious, and relaxing. Function is still the most important consideration, but water—and its consumption—is on everybody's mind.

Toilets account for about 30 percent of residential water consumption, and showers use about 37 percent. Add onto that the energy used by your water heater to maintain the perfect temperature for a long soak. Luckily, there are many fixtures and faucets on the market today that will give you the glamour and luxury you desire while helping to reduce your water usage and expenditures.

To find water-efficient products more easily, the Environmental Protection Agency (EPA) initiated a WaterSense program, which is designed to conserve the water supply by promoting efficient products. When you're shopping, you will see fixtures with the WaterSense label. These products, which are 20 percent more efficient than their standard counterparts, have met stringent standards backed up by independent testing before they are certified for high performance and efficiency.

But don't worry about sacrificing looks for function—in today's world you can have both. Fixtures and fittings that suit either your modern taste or your traditional leanings abound. You'll also be surprised to find them fabricated in materials you wouldn't expect to see in a bath and in finishes as glamorous as any baubles you might see on the red carpet.

Today's fixtures are heavily influenced by Modern European style. This bathroom, left and below, is an example of up-to-the-moment design.

3 mix and match

the top **10**
Fixture Amenities

1 eco friendly Fixtures that save water are a first priority. Look for the WaterSense label, which is an indication that a fixture is efficient both performance- and water-wise.

2 dual flush Toilets with a dual-flush feature have separate flushes for water and for waste, which makes them highly efficient.

2 dual-flush toilet

4 natural materials

7 mix and match

5 jetted tubs

10 hands-free

3 **euro styling** New inspiration from European designers is fostering a desire for interesting shapes and sleek modern styling.

4 **natural materials** Fixtures fabricated from natural materials, such as wood (especially teak), bamboo, and carved stone are gaining in popularity thanks to their Zen-like appeal.

5 **jetted tubs** There's no denying everybody wants a jetted tub. In fact, it's become a bathroom standard feature.

6 **spa showers** Spa features may include
- steam
- water or air jets
- acupressure massage sprayers
- aromatherapy
- MP3/MP4 or LCD TV input
- an integrated hands-free phone

7 **choice of water delivery** Take your pick from a variety of spout styles, including waterfalls, rainshowers, water tiles, handheld sprayers, or standard models.

8 **a thermostatic mixing valve,** or TMV, prevents bacteria growth and scalding by keeping water temperature above 140 degrees in the tank. Mixing it with cold water lowers the temperature to under 120 degrees at the faucet.

9 **high-style fittings** Sensuous shapes and chic finishes are a must at any price point.

10 **hands-free** It's all digital!
- preset water-temperature memory
- optional remote control

Soaking in Style

Soakers; whirlpools; classic claw-footed models; tubs for two; spas for four; contoured shapes, ovals, squares, or rounded tubs; streamlined or sculptured models; jetted tubs; tubs that offer a bubble massage; or a holistic-healing-inspired bath that incorporates sound, vibration, and chromatherapy. Hey, it's your soak, so have it your way.

Tubs can be custom made of stone, concrete, and even wood, but standard models are typically fabricated out of one of the following materials:

Fiberglass. Lightweight and moldable, a fiberglass tub is the least expensive type you can buy. But it's prone to scratching and wear after about a dozen years. Some come with an acrylic finish, which holds up against wear longer.

Solid Acrylic. A mid-price product, acrylic is more durable than fiberglass and less prone to scratching because the color is solid all the way through. Whirlpool tubs are usually made of acrylic because it can be shaped easily. It's also lightweight, an important feature for large tubs that can put stress on structural elements under the floor.

Cast Iron. An enamel-coated cast-iron tub will endure as long as your house stands. It's a heavyweight, though, and is not recommended for a large soaking tub unless there is adequate support.

The most common size for a tub that backs up against a wall is 32 × 60 inches, but you can find models in widths of 24 to 42 inches. If someone in the family is tall, no problem: you can purchase a standard tub that's up to 72 inches long.

A whirlpool tub built into a custom surround, above right, has the look and feel of luxury. But freestanding models can be pampering, as well. This 66⅜-in. soaker, right, has a silky smooth surface and sensuous shape thanks to the resin-based composite material from which it is molded.

do this... not that

not stone cold

If you are thinking about a stone bathtub—typically fabricated from solid marble or granite slabs—consider this: these vessels, as one manufacturer puts it, "seek the ambient temperature of the room." Therefore, the recommendation is to install a radiant-heat system in the floor rather than, say, a standard forced-air system.

Radiant heating can be installed in an existing home, but there are considerations, such as whether and how well the home is insulated and what energy source will be used to power it. It's best to consult a professional before making a decision.

Carved from a single block of solid travertine, this custom 22 x 60 x 60-in. "teacup" tub, above, offers the ultimate in luxurious bathing. Perhaps not quite as sybaritic, but also indulgent, is the teak-encased tub, below.

Bathrooms designed to please are those with high-quality fixtures and fittings that are both beautiful and reliable.

Far right: A glamorous, deep soaking tub is the focal point of this master bathroom, taking center stage in front of a windowed alcove. Separate lavs and vanities on either side of the alcove create perfect symmetry on this side of the room.

it's in the details *

Top: It's important to note the tub's pretty French-style "telephone" faucet. Its sprayer handle is both practical and charming.

Bottom: The glass-enclosed jetted shower features both a fixed showerhead and hand-held sprayers.

for freestanding tubs
@ www.kallista.com
www.porcher-us.com

Here's one bath you might call "the strong, silent type." Materials such as stone, glass, and metal combine in this minimalist design that is quiet and soothing.

Far right: The copper tub, which is extra deep for long, lingering soaks, has been encased in a stone-tile surround. **Top:** The tub's ledge remains free of all but a few items to maintain a spare look.

Bottom: A wavy etched-glass design forms the partition between the tub and a large walk-in shower.

it's in the details ✳

The same glass is used to enclose the rest of the shower, where showerheads and sprayers offer bathing customized to suit individual preferences and needs.

find metal tubs

@ www.neo-metro.com
www.palazzotubs.com

Praiseworthy Showers

The only thing limiting your showering experience is your imagination—and perhaps, your budget. You can customize your shower with all or some of today's pampering extras, including massaging jets, steam, natural light, and music.

Unless you're interested in a strictly no-frills unit, at least think about installing more than one showerhead and mixing and matching devices from any or all of the following three basic spray categories.

Fixed Spray. Mounted on the wall or ceiling, a fixed spray may come with a massage option. Rain bars and rainshowers pamper you with a soft rinse, while waterfall spouts deliver a soothing cascade of water. Another option, strategically positioned water tiles let you wrap yourself in water coming from all directions.

Handheld Spray. A handheld device is convenient for directing water where you want it. It stores in a wall-mounted slide bar that can be adjusted up and down to accommodate the tallest or shortest bather. Or it can be installed on the tub deck. Combine a handheld spray with a stationary showerhead, and then add a massager with multiple settings and a body brush, and you've created a custom shower environment that rivals any first-class away-from-home spa.

Jet Sprays. Just like those used in whirlpool tubs, shower water- and air-jet sprays are housed behind the shower walls. One manufacturer offers as many as 16 with its shower unit. Jet sprays can be programmed to various settings. Get a therapeutic hydro-massage to relax stiff neck muscles or a sore back, for example. If you like, select a full-body massage at whatever intensity is comfortable for you.

go green

MAKES (WATER) SENSE

An average household could save 2,300 gallons of water each year using a WaterSense-labeled showerhead. Any showerhead with this label is certified by an independent laboratory as meeting the Environmental Protection Agency's standards for efficiency and performance.

Twice as nice—this large custom shower has plenty of room for two.

A corner shower, above left, takes up little space in a small bathroom. If you've got it, flaunt it—multiple showerheads work on separate controls, above, allowing individuals to select their preferred water delivery. With the door open, it's like bathing outdoors. But you can have nature and privacy in this design, left, which is bathed in cheerful sunlight.

Cabin spa could describe the ambiance of this design. **Far right:** This custom-built stone soaking tub is part of could be called a "wet platform" that also contains an open showering area. The teak ceiling, matching a custom vanity (not pictured), pairs warmly with the cool stone surfaces.

Top: To enhance the theme, the homeowners selected pebble-tile flooring. A slab of stone from the property serves as a unique stair for stepping up into the bathtub.

it's in the details ✳

Bottom: In the large shower, separate showerheads and diverters allow two people showering together to choose their own water temperature and spray pattern.

Q&A

I'm doing a small bathroom renovation. My acrylic tub/shower is badly stained. Can I repair it or should I replace it?

what the experts say

Folks at the National Kitchen and Bath Association (NKBA) advise checking with the manufacturer of the unit. Sometimes stains are not as egregious as they seem. The NKBA also says, "If your unit is in two or more pieces, you may be able to replace only a portion of it. Normally, the tub is most likely to be stained." But if the problem is on the walls of the unit, the NKBA suggests replacing the wall section or tiling over it.

what real people do

A new tub isn't necessarily expensive, but once you factor in the cost of installing it (after removing the old one), you can blow a sizable chunk of your budget.

An affordable alternative is to install a tub liner. This involves applying a form-fitting acrylic sheet, or liner, over the old tub. The liner is fabricated from literally hundreds of molds made of old standard tubs. The installer takes detailed measurements of your tub to make a seamless match. Upon installation, a special adhesive binds the liner to the tub without disturbing the adjacent walls and existing plumbing. This type of refurbishing will stay looking good for years.

Another solution to minor chips or cracks in enameled or porcelainized tubs is reglazing, but it will not hold up as long as a liner.

A second bathroom may not require installing a tub, especially if space is limited. In this case, left, a walk-in shower serves guests well. Polished chrome fittings in the shower, above, suit the room's contemporary design. Built-in storage, below, keeps towels handy.

At Your Service

A rainshower showerhead (top) delivers a steady stream. Or suit your mood: flip down this rainshower panel (middle) to get a waterfall stream (bottom).

Tub and Shower Faucets and Fittings

Whether your style is modern or traditional, you can outfit your tub and shower with faucets and fittings to match. You can select from an array of trendy finishes—from polished and satin matte looks in chrome, nickel, pewter, brass, bronze, and wrought iron. For continuity, coordinate tub and shower faucets with those you select for the lav and with other hardware in the room. Many manufacturers make this easy for you by offering collections of matching pieces.

Most importantly, chose quality—inner parts should be made with corrosion-resistant brass or a brass-metal base. Also, be responsible, look for the WaterSense label, and buy a low-flow showerhead, which uses less than 2.5 gallons of water per minute (gpm). There are two types.

Aerating Heads. These are the most popular. They work by incorporating air into the water to form a misty spray.

Nonaerating or Laminar Flow Heads. These form individual streams rather than mixing air with water.

A reproduction of a antique design, the appearance of a "telephone" faucet, opposite and left, belies its updated technology. This innovative design, above, is a shower with a tub filler all in one unit. It's made of 100-percent stainless steel.

Lav Flair

Today's lav can be made of vitreous china, cast iron, enameled steel, fiberglass, acrylic (solid-surfacing material), stone, faux stone, metal, or even wood. Its finish may be hand painted, contoured, beveled, brushed, or polished. It can be a freestanding pedestal, mounted to the wall, or installed into or under a vanity top.

A vessel lav is an above-counter installation. But a lav that is installed into a vanity counter is described in one of four ways:

Self Rimming. The bowl of a self-rimming sink is surface-mounted: you drop it into the counter, and the ridge forms a seal with the countertop surface. This ridge or rim can be decoratively carved or handpainted.

Under Mounted. If you want a neat modern look, an under-mounted sink may be for you. In this instance, the bowl is attached underneath the countertop for a sleek, uncluttered appearance.

Integral. As the word "integral" implies, the sink and countertop are fabricated from the same material—stone, faux stone, or solid-surfacing. The look is seamless and sculptural.

Rimmed. Unlike a self-rimming lav, this type requires a metal strip to form the seal between the top of the sink and the countertop.

Rectangular vessel lavs on a spacious custom tiled vanity have a clean contemporary look.

Lavs come in all sizes and shapes. Two distinctly different vessel lavs, above and top right, sit on the counter. A pedestal sink, right, is a classic style that works especially well in a small room. An under-mounted polished stainless-steel bowl, below, is small but elegant paired with white marble.

smart steps Get the Best Buy

STEP 1 consider the options

If you are sprucing up an old bath or adding a new one in a house that you expect to sell soon, you might install fixtures with fewer bells and whistles. But if you are making a major investment, you will be happier in the long run with fixtures that may cost more but give you greater satisfaction for years to come.

Not sure about some deluxe features and whether they are worth the extra dollars you'll have to spend? Research product feedback on the Internet. Talk to your contractor, who may be familiar with it or can pass along critical feedback from other clients who may have purchased the same item or something similar to it.

STEP 2 go for quality

Sure, style and color are important, but it's just as easy to find a first-rate faucet that looks great in your new bathroom as it is to find one that looks fabulous but performs poorly. Always put quality first.

Ask the manufacturer about the expected life of the product and its efficiency.

Don't take advice from a store clerk unless he or she is an experienced remodeling professional.

You may be dismayed by the initial sticker price, but when you divide the cost of the product or material by its anticipated longevity, you may be amazed at how reasonable it actually is.

Lav Faucets and Fittings

For quality, inquire about the materials used for the faucet's innards. The best choices are solid brass or a brass-base metal, which are corrosion-resistant. Avoid plastic—it won't hold up.

Some of today's most popular designs come in polished or satin matte nickel, chrome, bronze, pewter, copper, and enamel.

There are three basic types of faucets for your consideration:

Center-set faucets have two separate valves (one for hot, another for cold) and a spout that are connected in one unit.

Widespread faucets feature a spout with separate hot- and cold-water valves. All appear to be completely separate pieces.

Single-lever sets have a spout and a single lever in one piece for one-hand control.

In addition, you may want to think about where you'll install your faucets—mounted on the wall, on the sink deck, or on the countertop.

When you are choosing a style, remember function. Cross handles are charming, but they can be difficult to grasp for the elderly, disabled, or very young. Levers and wrist-blade handles make more sense in these cases.

Always match metals. The brass finish on this high-arc faucet, above, coordinates with a number of styles, including the lav with which it is paired here. A one-piece single-lever faucet, right, conserves space where there is little or no countertop. A widespread set, below, has separate controls for hot and cold water.

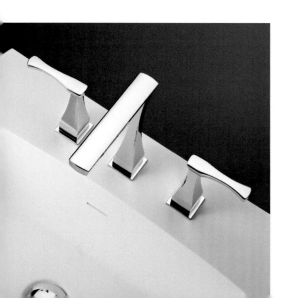

Antique bronze, top left, is a popular finish because it coordinates beautifully with earthy colored tiles and stone. Brass, updated in a matte finish on fittings and hardware, top right and above, adds a touch of refinement to a rustic look. A satin-nickel center-set design, left, features wrist-blade taps and traditional styling.

Today's Efficient Toilets

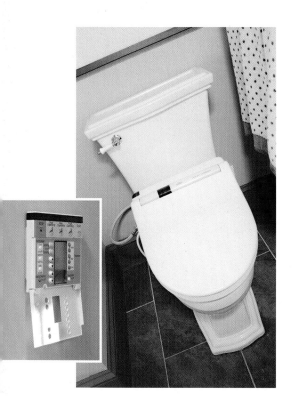

New toilets are more water efficient today. Vitreous china is still the material of preference, but there are more style options. Sizes are standard for the most part, but an elongated bowl will extend about 2 inches more into the room than a standard version.

The latest toilet technology includes the **dual-flushing system,** which gives you two flushing options: a partial flush; which releases a small volume of water for flushing liquid and paper waste, or a larger flush, which releases a greater volume of water for flushing solid waste. Dual-flush toilets use about 20 percent less water than standard toilets.

If it's not a dual-flush system, will you choose gravity or pressure to flush your new toilet?

Gravity Fed. This is the familiar device used by two-piece toilets. Press down the lever, and the force of the water that is released from the tank and into the bowl flushes waste away. But because today's models are restricted to 1.6 gallons or less of water, you may have to flush twice.

Pressure Assisted. This type uses water pressure in the line to compress air in a chamber in the toilet tank. Flushing releases the air, forcing water into the trap. This is a more efficient flush, but the toilets are noisier, more difficult to repair, and more expensive to buy than gravity-fed models.

A tankless "hatbox" toilet, above, uses a 0.2-hp pump for flushing. The model below contains a personal cleaning system with touch controls. Here's a one-piece lav and toilet, below right.

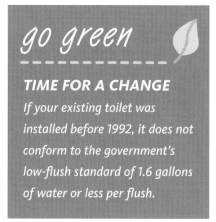

This bathroom, opposite, takes its style cue from the sleek, rounded lines in the matching suite of fixtures. When remodeling, always choose coordinated fixtures and fittings.

go green

TIME FOR A CHANGE

If your existing toilet was installed before 1992, it does not conform to the government's low-flush standard of 1.6 gallons of water or less per flush.

*do this...not that

to spend or not to spend

Take a trip to a home center, and you can find a new toilet for under $100. But should you buy it? Obviously, it's pretty standard looking—no fancy shapes or finishes, and there's nothing wrong with that. But price—in either direction—does not always guarantee satisfaction. Check out reviews that have been posted on the Internet, and ask your plumber whether he or she can recommend a reasonably priced and efficient model.

You have your choice of finishes when it comes to buying a toilet today. The two-piece model at right looks chic in copper. The stainless-steel bowl below comes in either a satin or a polished look. A hand-painted design distinguishes the model shown opposite top left. For the toilet shown opposite top right, you can choose between a cherry (pictured), bamboo, mahogany, or leather tank cover.

Leave no detail unattended. Look for a toilet lever to match the room's fittings. Some examples include wrought iron, right; brushed chrome, opposite bottom left; and satin nickel, opposite bottom right.

surfaces

t's not as simple as choosing a color. (And even that's not simple!) Making decisions about the types of finishing materials you'll use in your new bath is complicated. That's partly because, unlike color, wall tile, countertops, flooring, and other surface materials aren't that easy to change, and they cost a lot more than a gallon of paint. In this chapter, you'll find a fair sampling of what you can expect when you start shopping and advice for choosing materials that will serve you well.

It's great to have choices, but how to narrow them down? Start with what works best for you.

It's a Cover Story

So here's the scoop. Ceramic tile was once practically the only game in town, but now there's stone and all of its glorious variations, wood—yup, in the bathroom—glass in a dizzying array of colors, and concrete all dressed up with someplace to go, namely your bath. You've a lot to think about when it comes down to it.

There is also a remarkable assortment of materials, colors, and treatments in the synthetic category, including quartz composite, solid-surfacing material, and the familiar plastic laminate.

What's it going to be? Read on and take a look. Then you be the judge of what's best for your lifestyle, your budget, and your taste.

For visual interest in a monochromatic room, mix tiles of different sizes, shapes, colors, and materials.

1 natural materials

the top **10**
Surface Trends

1 natural materials In addition to stone, wood is gaining popularity in bathrooms.

2 glass In the form of accent tiles or as mirrored surfaces, glass is coming on strong.

4 porcelain tile

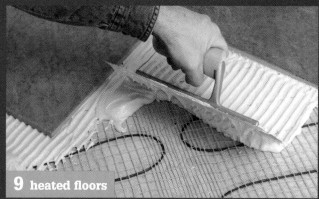

9 heated floors

3 quartz composite Actually, this surfacing material is 93 percent natural quartz. It is
- scratch, stain, crack, and heat resistant.
- resistant to most household chemicals.
- nonabsorbent, nonporous, and mold and mildew resistant.

4 porcelain tile A type of dense ceramic tile that can resemble stone. It can be glazed or unglazed, and it's practically impervious to water.

5 mosaic tile It's popular because you can get a big bang for your buck using even a small amount for a mosaic-tile accent in stone or glass.

6 integral surfaces Integral counters and sinks appear to be made from one seamless, solid piece of material and offer a clean, sleek look.

7 texture Pebble-tiled floors and walls have an outdoor quality that enhances a natural theme.

8 built-in antibacterial Some synthetic materials come with an antibacterial agent, built in during the manufacturing process, which will not wear away or wash off.

9 heated floors Technically *under* the surface, radiant heating systems are ideal with stone- or ceramic-floor installations.

10 "green" products Look for eco-friendly materials, such as recycled glass and bamboo, which quickly replenishes itself, for countertops, walls, and floors.

Stone, Wood, and Tile

Natural stone—granite, marble, slate, and limestone— may be the most expensive material you can choose for a floor or countertop. All types are extremely durable, but while granite and marble look refined, slate and limestone can have a more textured or rustic appeal.

Stone is a quality choice for a countertop or floor, not only because it is so durable, but because of the beauty of its grain and its natural colors. Finishes vary from polished (not recommended for floors) to honed, matte, and tumbled. No two pieces of stone look alike, so if you prefer uniformity, consider an engineered stone, such as quartz. (See page 112.) Stone is also porous and therefore must be sealed. If you're thinking about it as flooring, keep in mind that it can be cold and hard underfoot.

Granite may be showy or subtle, depending on its pattern. In this countertop, left, its rich veining enlivens an otherwise quiet design. Soft beige tones in the marble tile, top, warm a bathroom that has many cool surfaces. A slate wall, above, brings a sense of the outdoors into a room that has a dramatic lake view.

A dramatic wall of mixed-pebble tile takes nothing away from the modern look of this design.

Appealing Wood—A Warm Option

Wood in a room with so much moisture? You bet. If you seal it properly with one of today's high-tech finishes, you can use it safely and without the worry of mold, mildew, and warping. Underfoot, wood is more resilient and warm than stone or ceramic tile.

Keep in mind that some kinds of wood, such as teak, cedar, and redwood, hold up better than porous softwoods, such as pine. All wood, however, must be installed and protected properly. On floors, walls, or countertops, wood requires a polyurethane finish or, better yet, one of the newer sealants called "watershed protectors." But standing water can still mar a wood floor, so wipe it up immediately.

go green

A GRASS, ACTUALLY

Bamboo replenishes itself quickly, making it an eco-friendly alternative to wood. Use it on walls, floors, or countertops. If it comes prefinished, look for a low-VOC (volatile organic compound) rating.

This redwood-paneled bathroom, opposite and above, has a strong masculine quality. However, the homeowner wisely resisted wood and went for tile in the shower, where water will take its toll on even the most moisture-resistant species.

Ceramic Tile—A Classic Choice

Besides its practical features, including imperviousness to water, durability, and easy maintenance, ceramic tile offers the greatest opportunity to bring style and personality to your bathroom. Use it to add color, pattern, and texture to the walls, floors, or countertops. Enclose a tub or shower with it. Tile is versatile. It comes in a variety of shapes, sizes, and finishes. Use decorative tiles with hand-painted finishes or raised-relief designs to create a mural or mosaic.

Mix and match embossed tiles, accent and trim strips, edges, and a contrasting-colored grout (the compound that fills the joints). For long-lasting wear and easy maintenance, apply a grout sealer in areas exposed to water, such as the countertop, tub surround, or shower.

Watery green-blue subway tiles cover the walls from bottom to top in this bathroom, below and right. Ceramic tile is always a practical, good-looking choice.

The designer of this master bath chose porcelain tile to cover most of the surfaces in this room. Porcelain tile has a somewhat rugged and stonelike appearance. It's not only handsome, but it outperforms standard ceramic tile, having a water-absorption rate of less than 0.05 percent.

Far right: A granite countertop brings refinement and just enough of a bold pattern into the room.

it's in the details ✳

Top right: As you look into the room, you notice the different tones the designer used to play up the room's geometry.

Bottom right: Impeccably tight, even grout lines such as these are difficult to achieve with porcelain tile.

Glass and Concrete

It ain't got a thing if it ain't got that bling. So for ultimate glamour, glass is the one. Impervious to moisture, glass does not have to be sealed. However, you should seal the grout. As with ceramic tiles, glass tiles are not shatter-proof if something heavy falls on them, and they can be slippery underfoot. If you're going to install glass tile on the floor, make sure it is the type that is specifically made for that use; check the rating.

Glass tiles are luminous and gorgeous. They come in many colors and sizes; some have an iridescent finish. If you can do a large surface all in glass, use it in a border. Combine glass tile with a stone countertop for an ultra-luxe look.

A luminous wall of glass mosaic tile and a mirrored vanity make a handsome couple, below left. Light captures the iridescence of these opulent amber-tone glass tiles, below, while a simple mirrored wall, opposite, has understated glamour.

Surprisingly Elegant Concrete

This practical, seemingly plain material actually offers a world of decorative possibilities. What's more, it complements practically any style; it can look modern or rustic, plain or fancy. Concrete's surface can be colored, inlaid, formed into various shapes, or etched. Use it on a countertop, the walls, or the floor. But as with stone, concrete is hard and cold.

Concrete is not expensive, but for the best result, you'll have to hire a professional fabricator, which will drive up the cost, as will special stains and finishes.

Because concrete is porous, surfaces made with it require a sealant. But even when they are sealed, some concrete surfaces may crack. Make sure to check your fabricator's references, and ask to see examples of installations that have been in place for some time.

An integral sink and countertop molded out of concrete, opposite, has a seamless look. On this wall, above, concrete takes on the look of stone. In this unique setting, right, humble concrete looks magnificent.

I have recently installed large porcelain tiles on my new shower walls. What type of tile should I use for the floor?

what the experts say

Experts at the National Kitchen and Bath Association (NKBA) suggest using small tiles on the shower floor "for two reasons. First, because the shower floor must slope toward the drain." Large tiles would have to be cut to accommodate the angles that the floor will require in order to get it to slope. Second, "smaller tiles—and more grout lines—will offer better slip resistance in the shower," says the NKBA.

what real people do

The easiest types of small floor tiles to install come on a sheet. This is a relatively easy project for a do-it-yourselfer. One- or two-inch tiles that are attached to a 12 x 12-inch mesh-backed sheet let you get around corners and obstructions, such as fixtures, easily because you can cut the mesh or pull off a tile as needed. There is seldom a need to cut the tile itself, and you don't have to use spacers to create even grout lines.

Small black tiles set on the diagonal inexpensively dress up a field of plain white ceramic tile, left. This porcelain tile in a basket-weave pattern, above, comes in mesh-backed sheets.

*do this... not that

scrub or damp mop?

Is it crazy to install a white-tile bathroom floor? Won't it be hard to keep it clean? Not really, say most cleaning experts. The key is to routinely sweep it—or any floor for that matter—so that you don't grind in loose dirt. Then go over the floor with a damp mop. Forget harsh chemical cleaners that are not healthy for you anyway. If you sweep the floor regularly, and before a damp mopping, it will always sparkle.

Quartz and Synthetics

Quartz-composite material (often referred to simply as "quartz") is relatively new to the market. It offers the best of both worlds—the beauty and durability of natural stone and the easy maintenance of a laminate.

Composite material is produced by binding stone chips (typically quartz) to powders and resins to form an extremely durable product. Its textured and variegated look resembles stone, but the patterns formed are more consistent; patterns found in natural stone are random. Quartz comes in more colors than stone, too.

This material has also practical virtues. It cleans easily and is heat- and scratch-resistant. Because it is nonporous, it doesn't need to be sealed or polished for it to resist stains and retain its finish. You can use it alone or for an integral sink and countertop application. Price-wise, in most cases, quartz-composite material is comparable to natural stone.

Quartz complements other surfacing materials, such as ceramic tile. It can be used as an integral sink and countertop, with a vessel sink, below, or an under-mounted lav, opposite.

Solid-surfacing material comes in many colors, ranging from an assortment of neutrals to intense hues, such as the one selected for this countertop, above. This faux-stone shower and tub surround, left, is another solid-surface application.

Practical Synthetics

Solid-color-through surfacing material is a synthetic made of polyester or acrylic. It costs almost as much per linear foot as natural stone, but it wears long and well. **Solid-surfacing material** is impervious to water, and you can repair any dents or abrasions with a light sanding. Use it on the countertop and backsplash or for an integral sink and countertop application. Some types come with built-in antibacterial protection.

    Plastic laminate, on the other hand, is made of layers of melamine, paper, and plastic resin that are bonded under heat and pressure and then glued to particleboard or plywood. It's relatively easy to install and available in many colors and some textures. Lesser grades will chip and crack, so don't skimp.

This solid-surface granite lookalike, left, has been engineered to resist stains and scratches that can mar natural stone. You can use solid-surface material on the floor, too. In this bathroom, above, the designer created an inlaid pattern using it.

smart steps Before You Buy

STEP 1 weigh the options

Compare the advantages and any disadvantages of choosing one type of material over another. Things to consider include

■ **Cost.** For many people, this is the deciding factor. In that case, you need to know that natural stone will be expensive, but it usually pays back at resale time. In most cases, a synthetic material is more affordable.

■ **Care.** Okay, so you can afford to splurge on a gorgeous marble vanity top. But are you willing to routinely maintain it and treat it with TLC? Once again, an easy-care synthetic material is a practical alternative.

STEP 2 look for bargains

Shop around to get the best price. Visit several stores and showrooms, and look online. Be careful, however; there may be a good reason why two seemingly identical materials are priced differently. It may be about

■ **Quality.** It's easy to find products today that look upscale but are sold at bargain-basement prices. That's why you should never choose a product based solely on looks. Buy the highest grade you can afford.

■ **Brand.** You might pay more for a well-known brand. But usually the manufacturer has earned its high reputation and it will honor its warranties.

STEP 3 consider installation

Seriously, don't do it yourself, especially if you've chosen an expensive material, such as stone, or one that requires a trained fabricator, such as solid-surfacing material, quartz, or concrete. Manufacturers often will not honor a warranty if you fail to have their material installed by a qualified person.

Don't forget to consider the cost of labor in addition to materials. That's why a granite counter you thought was $50 per linear foot could actually cost $70 per linear foot *installed*. In addition to that, any special edge treatment you request raises the price even more.

STEP 4 try it out

How many times have you based a wall color on a paint chip only to find that what looked great as a sample looked hideous on the wall? If you're smart, you'll buy a small can of paint to try out the color at home before buying a couple of gallons. You can do the same with some surfacing materials, too.

Go to the manufacturer's or home-improvement store's Web site and look for interactive design guides. They will let you try out different countertop materials and colors in a virtual bathroom to see how they might look installed in your home.

Transforming a standard bath into a glamorous, pampering retreat is not always easy. However, this homeowner added class by choosing glass surfaces. **Far right:** In the tub area, a wall of glass tile features a custom mosaic made up of shards of blue glass bordered by iridescent tiles.

Top right: The same tiles are repeated in the border. You can see how the light picks up their rainbow of color.

it's in the details *

Middle right: Reflective materials increase the glamour factor in the room.

Bottom right: You can see the floor tile's colors reflected in the mirrored vanity cabinet.

find glass mosaic tile
@ www.mosaicsource.com
www.mglasstile.com

chapter 5
vanities & storage

n much the same way as kitchen cabinetry, the vanity and other cabinets in your bath will set the style in the room. In the past, unless you could afford a custom-designed vanity, your choice of standard bathroom cabinetry was limited. All that has changed. To get an idea of what you might like, visit bath-design showrooms and home centers to see in person what choices await you. Then think about how much storage you need and how much space you have for it.

When you're ready to furnish your new bath, choose a vanity and other storage pieces for style and function.

Practical and Beautiful

Dedicated bathroom storage has greatly improved in recent years. First, today's stock vanity cabinets have options for people of different heights. To further improve the storage picture, the vanity is often supplemented by additional cabinets, open shelves, and freestanding furniture. Even the medicine cabinet has increased in size and functionality. In fact, between the assortment of factory- and custom-made bathroom storage options today, there's really no excuse for cluttering the tub ledge with shampoo bottles and leaving towels on the floor. Available at home

A generous-size double vanity, below, makes it possible for two people to get ready for the day at the same time.

centers and large retail stores, stock cabinets can be inexpensive, as low as about $100 for a 36-inch-wide model. But check construction carefully. The same-size semicustom cabinet, generally available through showrooms, will cost at least several hundred dollars more. Custom units will be the most expensive, but they will be built to your specific needs.

If it's a master bath, you may want to splurge on upscale cabinetry. If you do, choose a comparable countertop, such as marble or granite. The same goes for a powder room. Because it's small, you may be able to afford something extra special—just think about how impressed your guests will be! If the cabinet is for a family bath that will get a lot of wear and tear, choose something that is durable and easy to clean.

The time to start planning bathroom storage is before you've actually begun the remodeling process. Start off by making a list of all of the items you will need to keep in the room, including extra towels, tissues, and grooming items.

Some stock cabinetry, such as this vanity, left, can be mounted on the wall at the most comfortable height for whoever will use it. Likewise, custom cabinetry, above, can be designed to the specifications of the homeowner.

I don't want to discover too late that I haven't adequately planned storage for my new master bath. How do I do it?

what the experts say

Designer Susan Obercian says, "Before I start design work for a bathroom, I have my clients answer a two-page questionnaire about their preferences for the new bathroom. This space is very personal, and everyone has their own wishes. That being said, of course, the size of the room will sometimes be the dictating factor for storage options. If space permits, a dressing table is a great place to store makeup, a hair dryer, and jewelry in a drawer.

A pullout pantry is a great way to store tall bottles of shampoo and such—and all are readily visible. A tall, shallow cabinet will hold an incredible amount of supplies. Towels can be folded in thirds if need be. A niche can be framed into a wall with glass shelves for powder and lotion storage. Medicine cabinets can be made to look like a framed mirror and are always useful. In a very small bathroom, the wall above the toilet can house a shallow cabinet. There is no formula. Each space has its own challenges. The trick is to be creative and, in a small bathroom, to use whatever "found space" you can.

what real people do

People who have never worked with an interior designer sometimes feel intimidated by the prospect, usually because they think it will cost too much money. But it's really more affordable than you think. For a modest (sometimes hourly) fee, a professional can offer you ideas and options you wouldn't know about otherwise, and they can help you avoid a costly mistake.

Planning storage and vanity needs is an important part of the remodeling process. This custom bath, left and below, was a collaboration between the homeowner and a design professional.

vanities & storage

Vanities

Choosing a vanity cabinet for your new bathroom deserves as much consideration as selecting cabinetry for a new kitchen. A vanity's function is twofold. First, it provides storage for everything from cleaning supplies to curlers. Second, it establishes the style of the room.

A custom vanity built to fit the space and your needs is one way to go, or you can purchase a stock cabinet, which you can customize with one of a number of finishes, a countertop of your choosing, and drawers and cabinet organizers. Interested in something more creative? Convert a piece of furniture into a one-of-a-kind vanity.

Once a dry sink, this antique cabinet, left, is a conversation piece in a powder room. If you need a large surface for cosmetics or hair appliances, choose a vanity with a long countertop and a single lav, above. A double vanity that is attached to the wall, opposite, keeps a small space from looking cramped.

Sizing Up Cabinets

Vanity cabinets are available in three ways:

■ **Stock.** Factory-made in a range of standard heights, sizes, and finishes, stock vanities are usually, but not always, the most economical type. Styles are limited.

■ **Semicustom.** Factory-made and outfitted with custom options upon your order—and usually midrange in price—semicustom vanities may include extras such as pullout bins, spin-out trays, special door styles, drawer organizers, and custom finishes.

■ **Custom.** Built-to-order to your bathroom's specifications, custom vanity cabinets can be designed by your architect, interior designer, or designer/builder. This is typically, but not always, the most expensive option.

Another "custom" option is the retrofitted piece of furniture. The piece will need some altering to allow for the sink and piping, and you should seal the finish against moisture.

A plain frameless-style cabinet maintains the simplicity of a Zen-inspired bathroom.

Vanity and Cabinet Dimensions

Stock Bathroom Cabinet Dimensions
(based on standard sizes in inches)

CABINET	WIDTH	HEIGHT	DEPTH
Sink base	15–72	28–36	16–21
Drawer base	12–21	31½–34½	21–24
Tall linen cabinet	9–24	83–96	21
Vanity linen cabinet	9–18	48–83	21
Vanity hamper cabinet	15–18	31½–33½	21

This custom-built piece fits perfectly into a space between two walls.

This spacious master bath has storage to spare.

Far right: Fine furniture details distinguish the custom cabinetry. A double vanity provides personal storage for each of the homeowners.

Top right: A glass-door cabinet separates the two vanities and stores shared items, such as hand towels and soaps.

it's in the
details *

Middle right: A built-in armoire serves several purposes, including linen storage. Behind one of the doors, there's an ironing center; the board drops down when the door is open.

Bottom right: A wire pullout bin serves as a hamper.

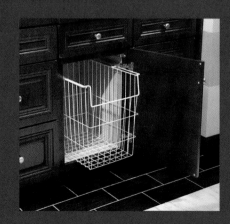

find storage systems
@ www.thecontainerstore.com
www.closetmaid.com

Style Matters

Vanity cabinets, particularly door styles, set the look of the room. There are two basic construction styles for stock and semicustom cabinets, framed and unframed.

Framed cabinets feature a full frame across the face of the unit. Hinges may or may not be visible.

Framed cabinets are usually more in keeping with traditional decorative styles, and the doors may have decorative panels and molding.

Frameless cabinets, which have a modern style, do not have a face frame. The doors are installed on the face of the box, and the hinges are hidden inside.

Frameless cabinets, opposite, have a sleek, unadorned look that goes with contemporary modern designs. Cabinets with a frame, above, are better suited to traditional styles, including Victorian, country, Old World, and cottage.

Bathroom Furniture

Spacious bathrooms, particularly in master suites, can be furnished similar to other rooms in the house today. Cabinets such as armoires and dressers, and even upholstered seating, may be part of the plan, thanks to finishes and fabrics that are able to withstand moist conditions. In addition, fine furniture details have upped the style quotient of even the most modest stock cabinets.

And if you like the idea of an antique but don't have one, you can buy a vanity that only looks like it was retrofitted from a vintage piece.

You can mix freestanding with built-in cabinetry as the homeowners did in this bath, below. An antique dresser makes a vanity unique, opposite.

Medicine Cabinets and More

Built-in lighting, swing-out mirrors, and three-way mirrored doors are some of the features you can find in a new medicine cabinet. In addition, some units come with a lock or a separate compartment that can be locked to keep potentially dangerous substances out of the hands of young children. If you don't have additional storage for bulky items, such as extra rolls of tissue, or appliances, such as a blow dryer or hot rollers, you can find cabinets that are made extra deep with such things in mind. Open shelving is another option, especially if you are short on space.

*do this... not that

storing linens

Whether you are storing towels in a linen closet or on open shelves, organize them by size and color. Do not store worn towels in the open; if they are that bad, it's time to buy new ones. Make sure the folded edge of each towel faces out, making them easy to grab.

These bathrooms, opposite top, above, and right, have both open and closed storage. The console only has a few small drawers, so keeping towels in the built-in is handy for both the lav and the bath. A medicine cabinet can be mounted on the wall, opposite bottom, or recessed into the wall.

137

Beautiful mahogany-stained cabinets transformed what was once a nondescript bath in an older house into a showplace. **Far right:** Custom vanities built into opposite corners make the most of the space. Joining them is a large dresser-like cabinet with drawers and shelves for storing bath towels and other linens.

Top right: You can see how neatly the cabinet fits into the corner. The vessel lav resembles a bowl sitting on top of the counter.

it's in the
details ✳

Bottom right: The position of the vanity left room for a heated towel rack next to the shower.

find bath cabinetry
www.kraftmaid.com
www.merillat.com

Above, a tiled niche between studs amply stores towels and more. A built-in cabinet, right, uses vertical space for linens and a hamper. Cabinets built around the toilet, below, can store tissue and cleaning supplies. A vanity drawer, below right, becomes more efficient with compartments for brushes and cosmetics.

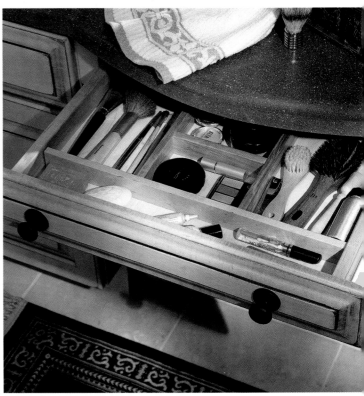

Linens and Things

Organization is key, especially in a small bathroom. So think about ways you can build in organization before construction begins and while you are thinking about the type of vanity you might be installing. Most household accidents occur in the bathroom, and so it's smart to plan how you will keep clutter off the floor. If a full-size linen closet is out of the question, make use of the space in the wall between two studs; this is a good place to install shelving. The toe-kick area under the vanity cabinet offers space for a shallow drawer, or it can store a collapsible slide-out step stool for children.

A freestanding antique chest is a helpful addition to the built-in vanity and cabinet, below.

STEP 1 analyze your needs

Make a list of who will use the new bathroom and how much storage they need. Besides clean towels, will you need a place for rolls of tissue, grooming and cleaning supplies, and small appliances?

If young children will use the use the room, plan a place to store bath toys—not on the floor where someone can trip on them. If they will be sharing the bath with adults, include a cabinet that can be locked, unless you can safely store medicines and other potentially harmful substances where children can't get access to them. Never store medicine on an open shelf.

STEP 2 divide and conquer

Make a plan now to store similar items, such as all bath towels on one shelf, all hand towels on another shelf. Keep grooming products and cosmetics together and separate from bathroom cleaners.

■ **Niches.** One way to stretch the storage capacity and compartmentalize it in a bathroom is to create recessed niches between the studs inside the walls. Locate them in different points of use, such as in the wall of the shower for shampoos, soaps, and shaving creams. Install another one near the toilet for an extra roll or two of tissue, or create one long niche for towels and a hamper.

STEP 3 accessorize

Some of the interior options offered for kitchen cabinets are available for bathroom vanities. Slide-out trays and lazy-Susans, for example, make it easy to find items that are stored in the back of the cabinet, and you can corral laundry in a roll-out bin. There are racks for everything from hairbrushes and curling irons to bulky blow dryers that you can mount to the inside of cabinet doors.

If you are ordering custom or semicustom cabinetry for your bathroom, you can also ask for compartmentalized drawers that can separate items such as cotton swabs and bobby pins from one another.

STEP 4 multiply

The vanity still reigns as the major supplier of storage in the bathroom. Because one height does not suit all, stock vanities now range from the standard 30 inches to 36 inches high. With two vanities in a shared bath, each one can be tailored to a comfortable height for its user. The 18-inch-deep units free up floor space while 24-inch-deep models store more.

If you have the space, consider installing additional cabinetry in the bathroom. If you don't want to go the custom route, you can find coordinated suites of stock cabinetry from the major manufacturers.

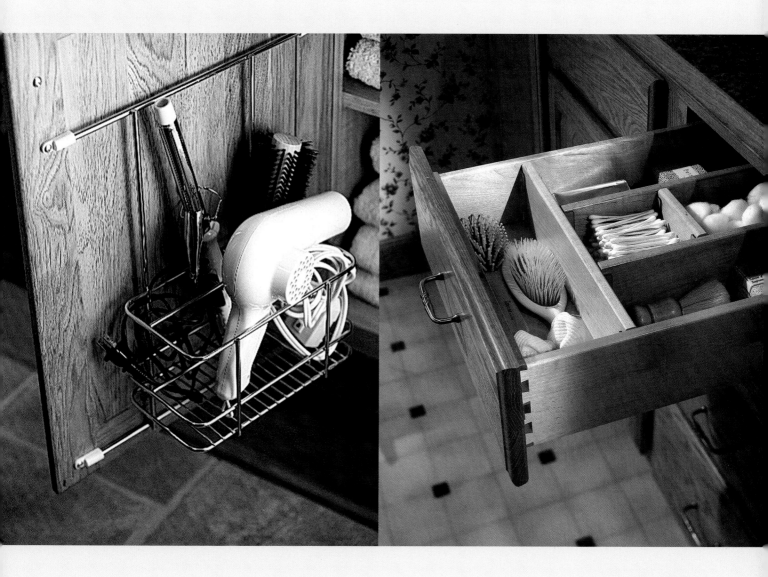

Dressing Rooms

Often part of a walk-in closet linked to a master bedroom and bath, a dressing room is undoubtedly a luxury that most people would love to have. If you're remodeling, sometimes borrowing space from an adjacent room makes adding a dressing room—or spacious walk-in closet—possible. If space is still tight, use pocket or bifold doors or sliding screens. You can use stock cabinets, but they should match or coodinate with the bathroom cabinetry.

This walk-in closet, right, has storage for special soaps, bath powders, and lotions. The owner of this impressive dressing room, below, gave up an entire room for storage.

In an open plan where the bath is visible from the dressing room, it's important to coordinate cabinet style.

light and air

The perfect combination of natural and artificial light, heating, and ventilation will keep your new bath beautiful, safe, and healthy for years to come. Understanding and planning light and addressing air-quality issues are not difficult, and taking the advice of experts won't cost you a fortune. Here's what you need to know to make your new space—and you—gorgeous and comfortable.

Good lighting and healthy air circulation are important factors in your new bath's design.

Natural Light

The most natural light source and the best complement to your bathroom is daylight—which means lots of windows. Not only does the room look better when it's bathed with warm natural light, but it makes you look better, too. What could be more invigorating than drenching yourself in sunlight as you take your morning shower? And as for relaxing, can you imagine soaking in a warm tub while you gaze at the stars?

Greatly enhanced glazing options and low-E glass have solved the problem of drafty, inefficient windows and the lost energy dollars associated with them.

If privacy allows, a large window, a bay, or a bank of smaller units adjacent to the tub will add to the luxuriousness of a bathroom. For homeowners who want to bring in more light but would rather not look at what's on view outside, a solution may be to install small windows high on the wall.

When you can't add a window, a vented skylight—also called a "roof window" —may be an option. In fact, skylights supply up to 30 percent more light than vertical windows. Better flashing systems have improved upon the old, leaky units of yesterday, and new technology has made skylights more energy efficient. Best of all, many newer models work by remote control for maximum convenience.

A large window next to the tub, below, is the only natural light source in this room. Adjustable window treatments, such as blinds, easily solve the privacy issue. Another way to brighten a bath is with an operable skylight, opposite, which also provides ventilation.

Glass block is one example of what is called a "fixed window," which means you can't open it. **Far right:** Here, it lets light into a bathroom and provides the required privacy. A fan takes care of the room's ventilation needs. **Top right:** A small round window on the other side of the room brightens a corner. **Bottom right:** Although this type of window is often fixed, this one is operable,

it's in the details *

pivoting out to allow fresh air into and bad air out of the room. Wall sconces and canister lighting supplement the room's natural light when needed.

find glass and acrylic block
www.pittsburghcorning.com
www.usblockwindows.com

Window Facts

Beyond the ubiquitous double-hung window, there are a number of styles from which to choose—and many come in standard sizes today. Replacing an uninspired unit with a graceful arch-top design, for example, is relatively easy and affordable to do. In fact, it's not that difficult to change the entire architectural look of your bathroom by replacing or adding windows. However, if you are going to do this, think about whether the style you plan to install is compatible with the rest of your house and how it will look from the street as well as from indoors.

If you want natural light to be part of your bathing ritual, consider the direction of the window in terms of the sun. Early-morning sun comes from the east; late afternoon sun comes from the west. If your window faces south, your bathroom will be sunny all day; if the window faces the north, you won't get much direct natural light at all.

get smart
SOLAR TUNNELS

What is a solar tunnel? It could be described as a tubular skylight, but it's actually a shaft that makes it possible to bring natural light into a room. In addition, solar tunnels are energy efficient and Energy Star rated. For the maximum benefit, locate solar tunnels where they will get the most direct light.

Casement windows with grilles, left, open vertically and are compatible with traditional architecture. Strong geometric shapes, such as this round window, above, are typical of modern design. This goes for strong horizontal lines, as well. The awning windows, opposite, which open outward, are an example.

Artificial Light

You will need adequate **ambient,** or general, lighting for overall illumination and suitable **task lighting** near the mirror for grooming. There are fixtures that are rated for use above a tub or in the shower; include these in your plan for safety. And for your senses, consider including accent or decorative lighting. **Accent lighting** draws attention to an interesting detail, such as a cabinet interior or a tray ceiling. **Decorative lighting** is mostly just ornamental, such as low-light pendants or sconces; if you install them with a dimmer, they may serve as both decorative and task lighting.

go green

TAKE A BREAK
Compact fluorescent lights (CFLs) are the most energy-efficient option. They cast a diffused shadowless light that is great for general illumination. Check your local code, which may mandate their use.

Whenever it's possible, it's ideal to position vanity lighting on either side of a mirror, left. A chandelier provides decorative light as well as some general illumination in this room, above. The fixture installed on the mirror, opposite, provides task lighting required for grooming. Aiming the fixture to cast light up rather than down on the countertop avoids glare.

Bathrooms have a lot of shiny surfaces that can cause glare, which you should take into account when you're choosing materials and planning lighting. **Far right:** These homeowners wanted the clean look of white in their master bath. White is highly reflective; in addition, the room is long and narrow with a bay of windows at one end.

it's in the
details ✳

Top right: Opaque bottom-mounted shades that diffuse glare are energy efficient and easy to adjust for cool nights or hot, bright days.

Bottom right: Lighting over the tub and shower is operated by separate switches.

Attractive Fixtures

Stick to a style and finish that is compatible with the other elements in the room. Coordinate the style of the sconces near the vanity with that of the cabinet, for example. These fixtures can put the final touch on your design, and today you can find anything from reproduction Craftsman style to lamps with a cylindrical high-tech look. Besides style, finish should play a role in your choice. Try to match a metallic finish with your faucets and the other hardware in the room.

If the room is large, combine more than one fixture type; if it is small, a ceiling fixture that includes a ventilating fan is practical. For accenting, pair uplighting fixtures, such as wall sconces, with downlighting types: recessed lights, pendants, or a ceiling-mounted fixture.

Confused? Ask the store's lighting specialist for advice. Show him or her your plans and samples of your colors and materials.

Ultramodern light fixtures for the bath have either a geometric or a commercial look. Small square "boxes" of light are positioned to complement the view in the mirror. To brighten a long mirror, a similar pair has been positioned vertically, above. Contemporary cylindrical sconces, opposite, have an etched opal-finish shade to soften the light.

I'm planning a makeup center next to the window in my bathroom. What type of lighting should I use?

what the experts say

"Lighting should be on both sides of the mirror—if it will fit—for face care and above the mirror for hair care," say the experts at the National Kitchen and Bath Association (NKBA). "These different light locations do not need to be on the same switch. There will be times when you only need side lighting."

what real people do

A bathroom that is very small may only have one light source. If that's the case, the light source should be at the mirror—ideally side fixtures that can serve as task lights and general illumination. The American Lighting Association says that you should "mount the fixtures 28 inches apart and 60 inches off the floor."

It is not a good idea to use a ceiling fixture alone because, although it can provide adequate overall light, it cannot offer the type of light that you need to apply makeup or shave at the mirror.

You need different fixtures for applying makeup and grooming hair at the bathroom vanity.

How to Look Your Best

Bathroom lighting should illuminate both sides of the face, under the chin, and the top of the head. Plan to use at least 120 incandescent watts. Never aim lighting into the mirror. If you use side sconces, position them no more than 60 inches apart, unless you pair them with another vanity light source. Ideally, combine side sconces with a fixture above the mirror.

If fluorescent side lights are mandated by your local code, install them up to 48 inches apart for sufficient lighting, and supplement them with recessed or surface-mounted ceiling fixtures. Use the deluxe warm-white fluorescent bulbs that more closely resemble natural light and provide good color rendering for makeup and realistic skin tone.

A double vanity, will require a different approach: treat each lav as a separate area, and light it accordingly.

A mirrored medicine cabinet, above, features fluorescent lighting on all four sides. A makeup area, right, benefits from shadowless light. Opaque glass shields the light sources, opposite, to prevent harsh glare.

Lighting Tubs and Showers

Light around the tub and shower area must be bright enough for safety and grooming. Recessed downlights or other fixtures designed for wet areas are fine. Shields eliminate glare, and shatter-resistant acrylic diffusers are safest. Any light fixture installed in a wet or damp area must be designed for such use. Your professional electrician will know how to handle the situation and can recommend the proper fixture.

According to the Lighting Association of America, "Lighting should be bright enough for cleaning, shaving, and reading shampoo labels. Choose recessed downlights designed for use in wet areas. Shielded fixtures will protect reclining bathers' eyes from glare.

"An adjustable accent light aimed from outside the tub is dramatic, glare-free, and great for those who bring books to the bath."

Whether you're taking a quick shower or a long soak, you need good lighting. Both the tub and shower have recessed lighting in this room, left. Even a small bath, above, benefits from more than one light fixture.

Decorative fixtures combine with practical recessed canisters to add drama and function to the tub areas in these bathrooms, above and right.

smart steps Plan Your Lighting

STEP 1 sketch it

Draw an informal lighting plan on paper. First, make a rough sketch of your bathroom's layout. Place your general lighting first, and then indicate where you'll need task lights. Start around the mirror. Plan lighting around the sides of the mirror for cross-illumination. This avoids the shadows that typically result from downlighting. Never focus a light to shine directly in the mirror or on a highly polished chrome faucet. The reflection of the bouncing light will distract your attention.

Decide on accent lighting—perhaps near the tub, making sure to follow local codes; don't place a fixture that isn't rated for wet areas too close to the tub.

STEP 2 visit showrooms

The best way to get ideas is to visit lighting showrooms and the lighting departments in home centers. This will give you a chance to take an inventory of fixture types and styles currently on the market. Also, you can take advantage of the advice of lighting specialists employed at these stores. Bring along your sketch. Some in-store advice is free.

There are also systems that computerize a variety of lighting options. A lighting specialist can design a program that sets the lights on a system devised for different moods and activities. Everything is preprogrammed and controlled by one central panel.

Clear the Air

Adequate ventilation is a must in any humid environment, and you can't get much more humid than the modern bathroom retreat.

Ventilation combats the steam and condensation that cause mildew, rot, and deterioration of the bathroom's surfaces and the surrounding rooms or exterior walls of the house. If you haven't installed a proper vapor barrier between the bathroom and the exterior wall, you may face serious structural damage in addition to peeling and chipping paint.

The simplest form of ventilation is natural: a window. If you don't have access to a window (for example, the bathroom is not located on an outside wall), consider a vented skylight or a roof window. Many come with electrically operated controls for easy handling.

In a multilevel house, you can install a shaft or tunnel that makes it possible to bring light and air from an operable skylight or roof window into a bathroom on the ground floor. Some of these units work by remote control for easy operation.

Hot air rises, and windows opened at the top, above left, make good sense. Like to take a steamy bath? Vent some of that humid air outdoors, left. Roof windows in this room, opposite, help to clear the air.

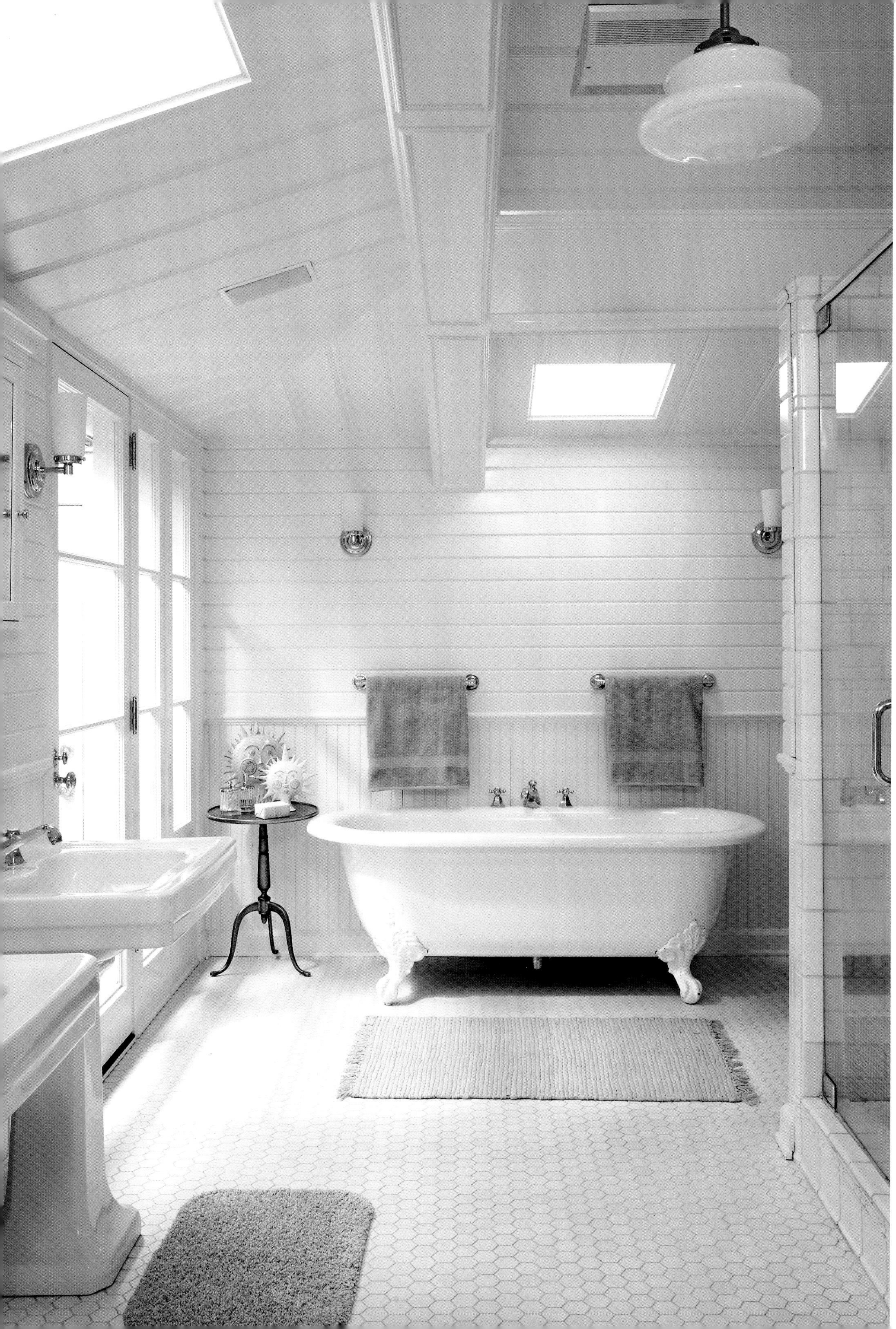

Ventilation Systems

In most jurisdictions, local building codes require fans in bathrooms that do not have windows. Even if you have access to natural ventilation, there are certain times you won't want to keep a window open (the middle of winter, for example). There are three types of bathroom ventilation systems available for your consideration.

A recirculating fan, as its name implies, moves the air around in the room. It does not vent air to the outdoors, but it does help to dispel some of the moisture that has accumulated on surfaces during bathing.

A ducted ventilation system discharges humidity in the bathroom by removing moist, stale air and odors and venting them through ductwork to the outdoors. If the unit is properly sealed, it will not bring outside air indoors. It simply clears the room of bad air and allows fresh air from the rest of the house to circulate into the bathroom.

Separate exhaust fans mount anywhere on a ceiling or outer wall of a new bathroom. The main thing is to connect the fan to the outside via a vent cap on the roof or sidewall.

do this... not that

choose the right exhaust fan

To remove moist air and odors effectively, don't skimp and choose a smaller, cheaper fan. Invest in one that matches the fan's capacity to the room's volume. Ventilating fans are sized by the number of cubic feet of air they move each minute (CFM).

Bathroom Size	Minimum Ventilation (CFM) Required
Less than 50 sq. ft.	50 CFM
50–100 sq. ft.	1 CFM per sq. ft. of floor space
More than 100 sq. ft.	Add the CFM requirement for each fixture: Toilet 50 CFM Shower 50 CFM Bathtub 50 CFM Jetted tub 50 CFM

Fans are also rated in "sones" for the amount of noise they produce. A fan rated at 1 sone is the quietest.

Even a bathroom with a window needs a fan, right. Here it's near the steamiest part of the room—the shower.

Keeping It Toasty

In addition to standard heating, there are options that can stand in for it or support it. **Radiant-floor heat,** for example, is energy efficient, invisible, and space saving (no radiators or baseboard heaters). The system uses hot water or electric wire coils installed underneath the floor. As the floor warms up, heat rises to take the chill out of the rest of the room. This may be a viable option if you are replacing a floor or building from scratch. Some flooring types may be incompatible with this type of heat. Good candidates include ceramic tile, stone, and wood.

Toe-kick heaters fit neatly into dead space under a vanity cabinet. They provide a pleasant blast of warm air on demand. Just flip the switch to turn cold tile floors toasty. Although electric heat sources can be expensive compared with other types, these devices aren't meant for constant use. In the long run, they shouldn't add too much to your energy bills.

Imagine wrapping yourself in a toasty towel to ease the transition from steamy shower to cool room. **Towel warmers** are becoming standard fare in bath design, particularly in master suites. There are two types: traditional hydronic radiator-compatible models, and those that work on electricity and simply plug into a wall outlet.

Using infrared bulbs that radiate heat into the space, **heat lamps** are usually mounted in the ceiling around the tub or outside the shower area.

A **convection heater** warms the air, and then circulates it using a small fan that is built into the device. Some come with exhaust fans and lights.

A toe-kick heater under the vanity cabinet, above, provides heat just when you want it. Many new master baths include this amenity today. A heated towel bar, below, is another feature that homeowners are incorporating into their bath for added pampering.

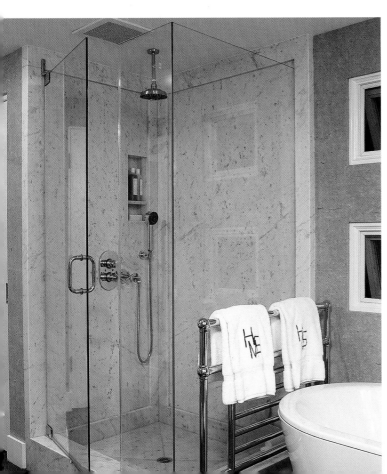

A gas fireplace insert in the wall near the tub is another option for keeping a bathing alcove comfortable on chilly days.

chapter 7
adding style

Decorating is one of the fun phases of your project. Remember, today's bathroom is more than utilitarian. In fact, it can be a showcase. If you're not sure about what you like or you're at a loss as to how to pull off "a look," here's some advice about how to create a cohesive decorative theme and a review some of the common elements that occur in today's most popular styles.

Throw out the rule book, and express yourself in color and design.

A Chic Retreat

A bathroom can actually be one of the chicest rooms in a house. In fact, a beautiful bath—whatever its size—is an important selling feature. But especially when you are renovating a bath for yourself, you should strive to give it style. Where to begin? Look at the architecture. Is it Modern or traditional? Even if the architecture is nondescript, you can introduce a style- or period-specific look using some of the same things you use to decorate the other rooms in your house—color, pattern, texture, and certainly, small details that add personality.

You may want to consult with an interior designer during this phase of your project. He or she can guide you and help you choose a color scheme, an overall look, window treatments, lighting fixtures, and other decorative details, such as art, for example.

But don't be afraid to go it alone. Forget about rules. Decorating is really about individual taste and choices. Do what pleases you and you can't go wrong.

*do this... not that

simple but not plain

No matter the size of the room, details pull the style together, and they often make the difference between a design that's nice but boring and one that has personality and polish.

Some of the best details you can include are the smallest—drawer pulls picked up at a secondhand store, an old bracket from an architectural salvage yard, or something as simple as a glass jar filled with seashells.

Less is more—at least it is here. This model of minimalism lets the materials and architecture speak for themselves.

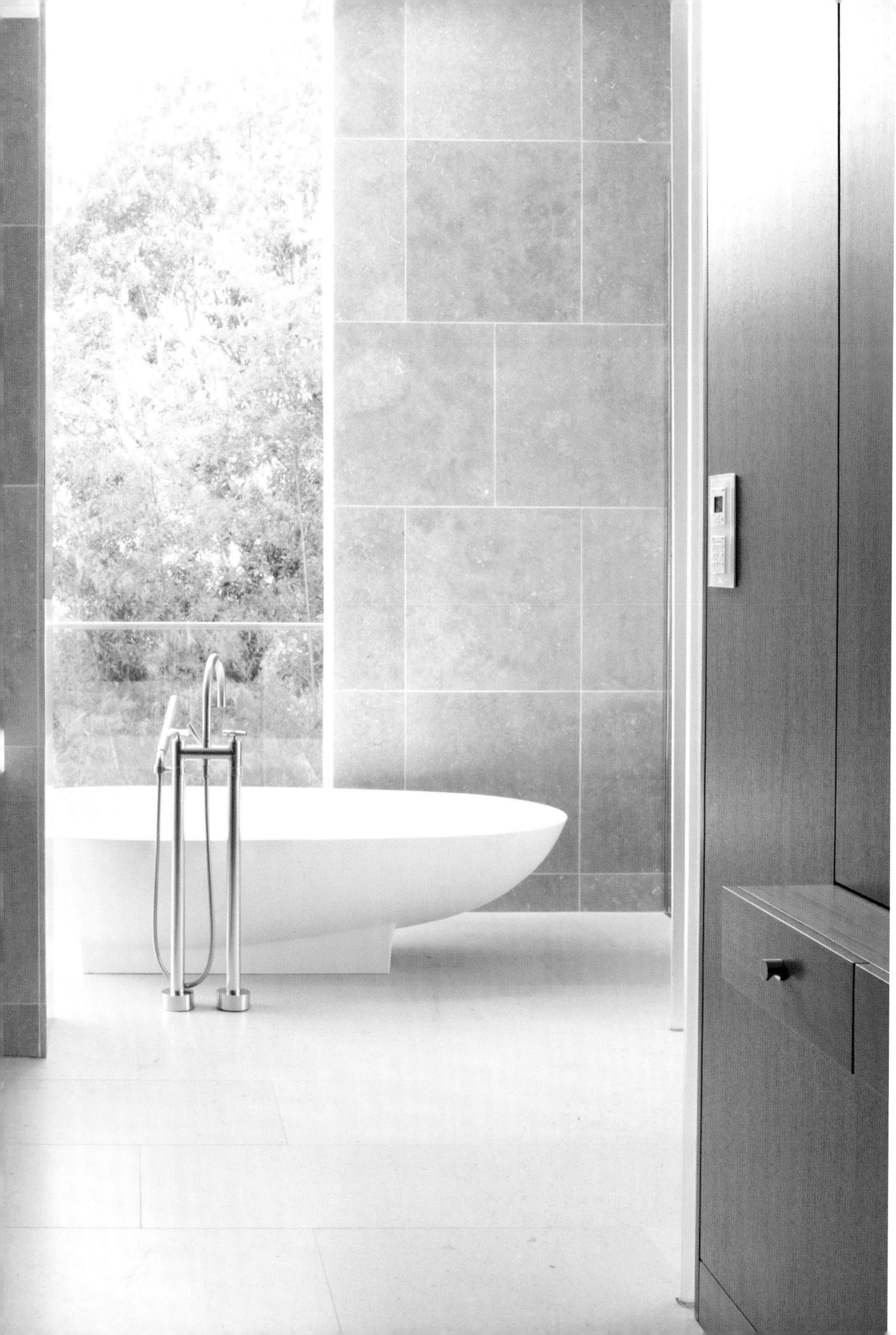

A Dip Into Color

Color has amazing properties. It can evoke memories, create a mood, or even change your perception of space. Light colors expand a room, while dark colors draw the walls inward.

Most people prefer to keep fixtures and permanent features, such as countertops, tile, and floors, neutral.

But you can introduce color to the walls or add it with accessories, such as artwork or even towels.

As a rule of thumb, use no more than three colors in one room. There really can be too much of a good thing. Use the colors in unique amounts and, perhaps, in different shades and tints. A monochromatic (one-color) scheme will produce a calming effect. When you use two or three colors, combine unequal amounts and

different shades of each one along with a dash of black, white, or another neutral. If you don't, your eyes won't know where to focus. Let one color dominate.

Where do you get your color inspiration? Forget about color fads. Look at the world around you. For an explosion of color, visit the produce aisle of the grocery store. Comb through fashion magazines and art books. Look at your own closet. See a repeated color? That's

a hint that you are naturally drawn to it. To test it out, pick up a small can of paint, and try it on the walls. Notice how color transforms the space. If you don't like it, paint is easy and inexpensive to change.

Blue stripes, opposite, make this wall look as crisp as a man-tailored shirt, especially with the white vanity and trim. A soft green, below, has a soothing effect on this room.

I like the way an all-white bathroom looks. Am I being a color coward? Can you give me any special tips?

what the experts say

"White comes in all sorts of shades, and there are countless variables in each one," says designer and color specialst Lucianna Samu. "In fact, some bath-fixture manufacturers offer no less than four variations of white; the difference between each one is nearly imperceptible.

"When you are choosing your white for the wall, trim, or even the ceiling, be sure to compare each varying shade the paint manufacturer of your choice provides. Take the time to do a swatch test on the wall. With some time, you will be able to discern between a crisp, cool white and one that is warm and glowing.

"All-white schemes are often impressive, particularly when some planning and effort are made to keep them that way."

what real people do

Homeowners often feel that white is a safe choice when it comes to a color scheme—even though, technically, white is the absence of color. But white can be hard to live with, considering the upkeep, especially in a bathroom. An all-white scheme can become grimey awfully fast. But if you're faithful about maintaining its pristine look on a daily basis, you shouldn't have to worry.

Sometimes people become bored with white, as well. Fixing that is easy. You can always paint the walls, add colorful artwork, or bring in color accents with a window treatment and linens.

Deep gold and red hues warm up and energize this bathroom, left.
A rich red complements the tile work and metal fixtures, above.

Traditional Looks

Today's traditional style has elements of English and American eighteenth- and early-nineteenth-century design. The look is rich and formal with architectural elements such as graceful arches, columns, trimwork, and double-hung windows with muntins or any divided-light window.

To create the look, select wood cabinetry, finished in a mellow wood stain or painted white, with fine details, such as fluted panels, bull's-eye corner blocks, and dentil and crown molding. The cabinet's door style

should be a raised-panel design. Hardware that evokes the mood of the period will add the right touch. Marble is a classic choice for surfaces, although some people prefer granite for the countertop.

An updated version of this look is called "transitional style." It isn't quite as formal, nor does it lean too much toward a contemporary look. If you're a middle-of-the-road type when it comes to decorating, blending elements of the past with those of today is your style.

Classic architectural features and elegant materials and cabinetry enhance the formal look of traditional style.

Elegant millwork transformed this space into a modern-day classic. **Far right:** An oval-shaped drop-in tub, ensconced in a light-filled alcove, is beautifully appointed with wood paneling, marble, and reproduction fittings. The wallpaper motif is subtle but adds just the right amount of pattern to make the large room inviting. **Top right:** Other formal details include the cream-color marble floor tiles and the trim

it's in the
details *

and molding. **Bottom right:** Custom cabinetry houses his and her lavs and storage. Linen-shaded sconces provide task light.

Feeling Nostalgic

all it cottage or Victorian, this look recalls the turn of the last century, with a bit of a modern twist. It's certainly much less formal and a lot less cluttered than its inspiration, but it still strikes a nostalgic look, particularly in terms of fixtures, cabinets, and hardware. A reproduction tub (often a clawfoot model), a pedestal lav, and matching fittings set the tone. Cabinets are painted, and usually white. The door style is typically flat panel—a simpler version of the type of door you'd expect in a traditional-style

room—and drawer and door hardware may be simple reproduction knobs in glass, porcelain, or metal.

For the walls, painted paneling—wainscoting and a chair rail, for example—or subway tiles can pull the style together. On the floor, small tiles—hexagon-shapes, squares, or basketweaves—evoke the era. If you prefer something warmer underfoot, use wood or a laminate look-alike.

A few contemporary touches keep a nostalgic look from becoming too cutesy. You could do this with a contemporary light fixture or window treatment. The key here is simplicity, informality, and light.

A reproduction tub and a "telephone faucet," and the room's white-painted paneled walls create a pleasantly nostalgic look in this room, left. A pedestal sink, above, evokes a Victorian mood.

Feeling Nostalgic **187**

This pretty room has views of and access to a private garden and is flooded with light all day.

Far right: A pair of pedestal sinks and the floor tile establish the cottage theme. Sconces and art add a couple of contemporary notes. **Top right:** A beautiful clawfoot tub, an exact reproduction of a turn-of-the-last-century model, is the room's centerpiece. The white painted bead-board wainscot is another period detail. White paint unites the horizontal wide-plank

it's in the
details ✳

paneling on the upper walls and ceiling. **Bottom right:** Bath mats and towels bring outdoor color inside.

In a Modern Mood

You may often see the words "modern" and "contemporary" used interchangeably. But to be precise, Modern is a style unto itself with roots in the early to mid-twentieth century. It's sparce—no Victorian frills—sleek, geometric, and somewhat high-tech. Contemporary actually refers to what is of the moment—the style of *now*.

If you like clean lines and a minimum of ornamentation, you are a Modernist. The architecture is spare and right-angled—no decorative trimwork or graceful arches. Materials tend to be industrial—metal and glass—but contemporary interpreters of the style have added warmth, using some color and wood to make the look less severe. Cabinets without a face frame and with flat-panel doors and drawers fill the bill in medium to deep finishes.

Casement or awning windows without grilles are compatible with a Modern interior, and window treatments are minimal if at all. All types of natural stone, concrete, and synthetic materials work well with this style.

Glass and stone are warmed by the mid-tone wood in this Modern bath, below left and right and opposite. The beauty of this design lies in the architecture and the materials sans ornament.

This master bath is a worthy twenty-first-century interpretation of Modern design. **Far right:** Above the vanity, with its polished limestone counter, a striking ebony-colored recessed wall is the backdrop for simple faucets and unframed mirrors that hang from metal rods. The compact fluorescent light fixtures have been mounted directly on the glass. **Top right:** The bath fittings, which have been

it's in the details ✳

mounted on the tub's limestone deck, continue the minimalist theme. **Bottom right:** Sea-green glass and limestone tiles in the walk-in shower add subdued color.

Asian Influences

Near Eastern and Far Eastern cultures are having a notable effect on Western design. And no place around the house exemplifies this trend more than the bathroom—the home spa or the personal retreat. One way to create an Eastern ambiance in your bath is with color. The most bedazzling colors— the brightest blue, red, yellow, and purple—are the most popular in the Near East. They can be spectacular in a jewel-box-like powder room. But if your aim is for a calmer, more Zen-like ambiance, you'll need to tone

This less-is-more design, left, hints at Zen-inspired style in the calm green color of the walls and the bamboo shade. There are evocations of the Near East in these bright-red walls and the bamboo console and frames, above. A Japanese-style soaking tub, textured walls, and quiet lighting, opposite, create a calming retreat.

down the palette to softer, nature-inspired colors.

Texture is another important element. You can add it with a textured wallcovering that resembles natural grasscloth (the real thing being too delicate for a steamy bathroom) or a textured paint treatment.

Bamboo is a material that always evokes the East and it's an excellent flooring choice. For the windows or doors, consider Shoji screens or natural wood or bamboo shades.

Keep the room simple, but add one or two accents such as tatami mats, a meditation gong, or a small indoor water feature to enhance the mood.

A blend of Asian and Modern decor, this master bath is a good example of what is called "Fusion design."

Far right: A wall of Shoji screens is the focal point of the room, made more dramatic by the diffused lighting that draws your eye to this feature. The room's neutral color scheme is quiet and calming.

Top right: A mirrored wall visually enlarges the space.

it's in the
details ✳

The vanity's spare Modern looks pair well with the Asian influences in the room.

Bottom right: Shoji screens slide open to reveal storage and a dressing room.

Old World Classics

Neoclassical, or Old World, style mimics ancient Roman and Greek design. It developed in the late-eighteenth to mid-nineteenth century upon the excavation of the ruins of Pompeii. It was highly influential on architecture and furniture design of that era, including Federal and Empire styles. Today's version incorporates classic architectural and design themes, including columns, pediments, ornate carvings and plasterwork, curvaceous shapes, and decorating motifs such as urns, scrolls, and shield shapes. It is highly ornamental.

To achieve this opulent look, select formal-style wood cabinetry with heavy carving and ornate molding. Lavish the scheme with rich finishing details, such as stone floors, walls, and countertops. Take your color cues from the tones in the wood and the stone, the warm sunny climate of southern Europe, and the deep aquamarine hues of the Mediterranean and the Aegean seas.

Handsome slate tiles in warm chocolate, gray, and umber inspired the color scheme in this Old World design, below. The tiled arched entry into the walk-in shower, right, is a throwback to ancient architecture.

O ld World meets New World in this artful Southern California master retreat. The room is reminiscent of the old monastaries that once lined the coast. **Far right:** A stained-glass window in the open shower and bath area is an antique. Stone-tile walls convey the sense of an old European structure.

Top right: The smoky glass wall reveals downlit niches holding carved Mexican folk art and a downlit retablo.

it's in the
details ✳

Bottom right: Antique Mexican furnishings serve the design well. A chest retrofitted with a vessel sink makes a unique vanity.

STEP 1 make a sample board

Try out your ideas on a sample board first. To make one, use a 2 x 4-foot sheet of ½-inch plywood, which is heavy enough to hold your samples but light enough for you to handle. Mount the samples on the board. Include paint chips, fabric swatches, flooring and tile samples, countertop chips—even the color of the linens. The board lets you test ideas before you start buying materials and make costly mistakes. Try different combinations of colors and patterns. Look at them under all types of light, night and day. Add photographs of fixtures, fittings, and vanities, and record manufacturer and retail sources, too.

STEP 2 note your sight lines

A sight line is the visual path the eye follows from a given point within a room or from an entrance. A room's primary sight line is at the entry. It is the most important one because it draws your attention into the room. Your eye immediately moves in one direction toward whatever is directly opposite the doorway. Very often in a bathroom that focus will be the tub or a good-looking vanity. If your sights lines are bad, the time for relocating fixtures is not at the decorating stage. However, if you're still in the planning process, rethink your floor plan to see what you may be able to move.

resource guide

The following list of manufacturers and associations is meant to be a general guide to additional industry and product-related sources. It is not intended as a listing of products and manufacturers represented by the photographs in this book.

MANUFACTURERS

Accessible Environments, Inc.
800-643-5906
www.acessinc.com
Sells handicap-accessible products.

Alchemy Glass
877-552-5243
www.alchemy-glass.com
Manufactures glass sinks, countertops, mirrors, and light fixtures.

American Standard
800-442-1902
www.americanstandard-us.com
Manufactures plumbing and tile products.

Ann Sacks Tile and Stone
part of the Kohler Company
800-278-8453
www.annsacks.com
Manufactures a broad line of tile and stone, including terra-cotta and mosaics.

Armstrong World Industries
717-397-0611
www.armstrong.com
Manufactures floors, cabinets, and ceilings for both residential and commercial use.

Artemide
631-694-9292
www.artemide.com
Manufactures lighting fixtures.

Artistic Tile
877-528-5401
www.artistictile.com
Offers different types of tile, including those made of stone, ceramic, glass, metal, cement, and cork.

BainUltra (also known as Ultra Bath)
800-463-2187
www.ultrabath.com
Manufactures a luxury line of bathtubs that offer a hydro-therapeutic massage.

Bemis Manufacturing Co.
800-558-7651
www.bemismfg.com
Manufactures toilet seats.

Benjamin Moore & Co.
www.benjaminmoore.com
Manufactures paint.

CaesarStone USA
818-779-0999
www.caesarstoneus.com
Manufactures quartz-composite countertops.

Carrara Tiles
888-422-4655
www.carraratiles.com
Distributes slate and granite slabs and tile.

CertainTeed
800-233-8990
www.certainteed.com
Manufactures building products.

ClosetMaid

800-874-0008

www.closetmaid.com

Produces home storage and organization systems.

The Container Store

888-266-8246

www.thecontainerstore.com

Sells storage and organization products.

Contrast Lighting

888-839-4624

www.contrastlighting.com

Manufactures recessed lighting, suspension lamps, and wall and ceiling fixtures.

Cooper Lighting

www.cooperlighting.com

Manufactures lighting products.

Corian, a div. of DuPont

800-441-7515

www.corian.com

Manufactures solid-surfacing material for residential and commercial kitchens.

Dal-Tile

214-398-1411

www.daltile.com

Manufactures ceramic and stone tile.

Dex Industries

404-753-0600

www.dexstudios.com

Creates custom concrete sinks and countertops.

eFaucets

800-891-0896

www.efaucets.com

Online retailer of bathroom and kitchen faucets, sinks, and accessories.

Formica Corp.

800-367-6422

www.formica.com

Manufactures plastic laminate and solid-surfacing material.

Ginger

www.gingerco.com

Manufactures lighting and bathroom accessories.

Herbeau Creations of America

239-417-5368

www.herbeau.com

Makes vitreous-china fixtures.

Hoesch Design

www.hoesch.de

Manufactures tubs and shower partitions.

Hunter Douglas

1-800-789-0331

www.hunterdouglas.com

Manufactures custom-made window treatments.

Jaclo

800-852-3906

www.jaclo.com

Manufactures showerheads and body sprays.

Jacuzzi Whirlpool Bath

www.jacuzzi.com

Manufactures jetted tubs and showers.

Kallista

888-4-52554782

www.kallista.com

Manufactures plumbing products such as faucets, showerheads, and sinks.

Kichler Lighting

866-558-5706

www.kichler.com
Manufactures decorative light fixtures, lamps, and home accessories.

Kohler
800-456-4537
www.kohlerco.com
Manufactures kitchen and bath sinks, faucets, and related accessories.

KraftMaid Cabinetry
888-562-7744
www.kraftmaid.com
Manufactures stock and built-to-order cabinets with a variety of finishes and storage options.

Lasco
800-945-2726
www.lascobathware.com
Makes barrier-free showers.

Lightolier
800-215-1068
www.lightolier.com
Manufactures lighting fixtures.

Lightology
773-883-6111
www.lightology.com
Manufactures lighting fixtures.

Maestro Mosaics
312-670-4400
www.mglasstile.com
Supplies and installs stone and glass tile.

Majestic Shower Co.
800-675-6225
www.majesticshower.com
Manufactures showers and glass-door enclosures.

Mannington, Inc.
800-356-6787
www.mannington.com
Manufactures residential and commercial flooring products.

Mansfield Plumbing Products
877-850-3060
www.mansfieldplumbing.com
Manufactures toilets, lavs, bathtubs, and whirlpools.

Minka Group
951-735-9220
www.georgekovacs.com
Designs contemporary lighting products.

MGS Progetti
www.mgsprogetti.com
Manufactures stainless-steel faucets.

Merillat
www.merillat.com
Manufactures cabinets.

Moen
440-962-2000
www.moen.com
Manufactures faucets, sinks, and accessories for both kitchens and baths.

Mosaic Source
562-598-3143
www.mosaicsource.com
Online source for mosaic and recycled-glass tiles.

Motif Designs
800-431-2424
www.motif-designs.com
Manufactures furniture, fabrics, and wallcoverings.

Mr. Sauna, Inc., and Mr. Steam, Inc.
part of the Sussman Lifestyle Group
800-767-8326
www.mrsauna.com, www.mrsteam.com
Manufactures saunas and sauna products.

Nantucket Beadboard
603-330-1070
www.beadboard.com
Manufactures bead-board products.

Neo-Metro, a div. of Acorn Engineering Co.
800-591-9050
www.neo-metro.com
Manufactures countertops, tubs, lavs, and tile.

Neptune
U.S.: 888-226-7899
C.A.: 888-226-7099
www.bainsneptune.com
Manufactures bathtubs and showers.

NuTone, Inc.
888-336-3948
www.nutone.com
Manufactures ventilation fans, medicine cabinets, and
lighting fixtures.

Palazzo Tubs
813-625-1178
www.palazzotubs.com
Manufactures luxury tubs.

Pfister Faucets
1-800-732-8238
www.pfisterfaucets.com
Manufactures faucets.

Pittsburgh Corning
800-871-9918
www.pittsburghcorning.com

Manufactures glass blocks, shower systems, and
windows.

Porcelanosa
201-995-1310
www.porcelanosa-usa.com
Manufactures marble and tile surfaces and mosaics.

Porcher
800-359-3261
www.porcher-us.com
Manufactures luxury plumbing fixtures.

Radiantec
www.radiantec.com
Manufactures radiant-heating systems.

Robern, a div. of Kohler
800-877-2376
www.robern.com
Manufactures medicine cabinets and accessories.

Saunatec
888-780-4427
www.saunatec.com
Manufactures saunas, steam baths, sauna heaters, and
other luxury bath items.

Seagull Lighting Products, Inc.
800-877-4855
www.seagulllighting.com
Manufactures lighting fixtures.

Sherwin-Williams
www.sherwin-williams.com
Manufactures paint.

Schonbek Worldwide Lighting, Inc.
800-836-1892
www.schonbek.com
Manufactures crystal lighting fixtures.

Solar Screen

866-230-4700

www.northsolarscreen.com

Manufactures energy-efficient window shades.

Sonia

www.sonia-sa.com

Manufactures bath fixtures.

Sonoma Cast Stone

877-939-9929

www.sonomastone.com

Designs and builds concrete sinks and countertops.

Sterling Plumbing

800-783-7546

www.sterlingplumbing.com

Offers ADA-compliant bathroom products.

Stone Forest

888-682-2987

www.stoneforest.com

Manufactures metal and stone bathtubs and lavs.

Thibaut Inc.

800-223-0704

www.thibautdesign.com

Manufactures wallpaper and fabrics.

Toto USA

770-282-8686

www.totousa.com

Manufactures toilets, bidets, sinks, and bathtubs.

US Block Windows

888-256-2599

www.usblockwindows.com

Manufactures acrylic and glass-block windows.

Velux-America

www.velux.com

Manufactures skylights and solar tunnels.

Villeroy and Boch

877-505-5350

www.villeroy-boch.com

Manufactures china fixtures.

Vitra USA

770-904-6830

www.vitra-usa.com

Manufactures products and accessories for the bath.

Waterworks

800-899-6757

www.waterworks.com

Manufactures plumbing products.

Wetstyle

866-842-1367

www.wetstyle.ca

Manufactures bath fixtures.

Whirlpool Corp.

866-698-2538

www.whirlpool.com

Manufactures major home appliances.

Wilsonart International, Inc.

800-433-3222

www.wilsonart.com

Manufactures solid-surfacing material; plastic laminate; and adhesive for countertops, cabinets, floors, and fixtures.

Wood-Mode Fine Custom Cabinetry

877-635-7500

www.wood-mode.com

Manufactures semicustom cabinetry.

York Wallcoverings

717-846-4456

www.yorkwall.com

Manufactures a wide variety of wallpapers and borders; offers online decorating tips and advice.

Zodiaq, a div. of DuPont
800-441-7515
www.zodiaq.com
Manufactures quartz-composite countertops.

ASSOCIATIONS

American Institute of Architetcts (AIA)
800-242-3837
www.aia.org
A professional membership organization for licensed architects, emerging professionals, and allied partners.

American Society of Interior Designers (ASID)
202-546-3480
www.asid.org
A community committed to interior design and its positive effect on people's lives.

Ceramic Tile Institute of America (CTIOA)
310-574-7800
www.ctioa.org
A trade organization that promotes the ceramic tile industry. Its Web site provides consumer information about ceramic tile.

Forest Stewardship Council of the United States (FSCUS)
612-353-4511
www.fscus.org
A professional organization coordinating the development of forest-management standards.

International Interior Design Association (IIDA)
888-799-4432
www.iida.org
A professional organization facilitating a community of interior design professionals.

National Association of Remodeling Industry (NARI)
800-611-6274
www.nari.org
A professional organization for remodelers, contractors, and design/remodelers; also offers consumer information.

National Kitchen and Bath Association (NKBA)
800-843-6522
www.nkba.org
A national trade organization for kitchen and bath design professionals; offers consumers product information and a referral service.

Tile Council Of America
864-646-8453
www.tileusa.com
A trade organization dedicated to promoting the tile industry; also provides consumer information on selecting and installing tile.

DESIGNERS

Helene Goodman, IIDA
Interior Design
723-747-8502
hgoodman@comcast.net

Susan Obercian
European Country Kitchens
973-218-9004
www.eckitchens.com

Lucianna Samu
www.reallyathome.com
lu@luciannasamu.com

glossary

Absorption (light): The energy (wavelengths) not reflected by an object or substance. The color of a substance depends on the wavelength reflected.

Accent lighting: A type of light that highlights an area or object to emphasize that aspect of a room's character.

Accessible design: Design that accommodates persons with physical disabilities.

Accessories: Towel racks, soap dishes, and other items specifically designed for use in the bath.

Adaptable design: Design that can be easily changed to accommodate a person with disabilities.

Ambient light: General illumination that fills a room. There is no visible source of the light.

Antiscalding valve (pressure-balancing valve): A single-control fitting that contains a piston that automatically responds to changes in line water pressure to maintain temperature; the valve blocks an abrupt drop or rise in temperature.

Apron: The front extension of a bathtub that runs from the rim to the floor.

Awning window: A window with a single framed-glass panel. It is hinged at the top to swing out when it is open.

Backlighting: Illumination coming from a source behind or at the side of an object.

Backsplash: The finish material that covers the wall behind a countertop. The backsplash can be attached to the countertop or separate from it.

Barrier-free fixtures: Fixtures specifically designed for disabled individuals who use wheelchairs or who have limited mobility.

Baseboard: A trim board attached as part of a base treatment to the bottom of a wall where it meets the floor.

Base cabinet: A cabinet that rests on the floor under a countertop or vanity.

Base plan: A map of an existing bathroom that shows detailed measurements and the location cf fixtures and their permanent elements.

Basin: A shallow sink.

Bidet: A bowl-shaped fixture that supplies water for personal hygiene. It looks similar to a toilet.

Blanket insulation: Flexible insulation, such as fiberglass or mineral wool, which comes packaged in long rolls.

Blocking: A small piece of wood used to reinforce framing members.

Bridging: Lumber or metal installed in an X-shape between floor joists to stabilize and position the joists.

Built-in: A cabinet, shelf, medicine chest, or other storage unit that is recessed into the wall.

Bump out: Living space created by cantilevering the floor and ceiling joists (or adding to a floor slab) and extending the exterior wall of a room.

Cable: One or more wires enclosed in protective plastic or metal sheathing.

Candlepower (Cp): The intensity of light measured at the light source.

Cantilever: A structural beam supported on one end. A cantilever can be used to support a bump out.

Casement window: A window that consists of one framed-glass panel that is hinged on the side. It swings outward from the opening at the turn of a crank.

Casing: The general term for any trim that surrounds a window.

Cement-based backer board: A rigid panel designed for use as a substrate for ceramic tiles in wet areas.

Centerline: The dissecting line that runs through the center of an object, such as a sink.

CFM: An abbreviation that refers to the amount of cubic feet of air that is moved per minute by an exhaust fan.

Chair rail: A decorative wall molding installed midway between the floor and ceiling. Traditionally, chair rails protected walls from damage from chair backs.

Cleanout: A removable plug in a trap or drainpipe, which allows easy access for removing blockages.

Clearance: The amount of space between two fixtures, the centerlines of two fixtures, or a fixture and an obstacle, such as a wall. Clearances may be mandated by building codes.

Cleat: A piece of lumber fastened —to a joist or post, for example— as a support for other lumber.

Closet bend: A curved section of drain beneath the base of a toilet.

Closet flange: The rim of a closet bend used to attach the toilet drainpipe to the floor.

Code: A locally or nationally enforced mandate regarding structural design, materials, plumbing, or electrical systems that states what you can or cannot do when you build or remodel. Codes are intended to protect standards of health, safety, and land use.

Color rendition index (CRI): Measures the way a light source renders color. The higher the index number, the closer colors illuminated by the light source resemble how they appear in sunlight.

Combing: A painting technique that involves using a small device with teeth or grooves over a wet painted surface to create a grained effect.

Contemporary style: A style of decoration or architecture that is modern and pertains to what is current.

Cornice: Any molding or group of moldings used in the corner between a wall and a ceiling.

Correlated color temperature (CCT): A value assigned to a fluorescent lamp indicating the warmth or coolness of the light it produces.

Countertop: The work surface of a counter, usually 36 inches high. Common countertop materials include stone, plastic laminate, ceramic tile, concrete, and solid surfacing.

Cove lights: Lights that reflect upward, sometimes located on top of wall cabinets.

Crown molding: A decorative molding usually installed where the wall and ceiling meet.

Dimmer switch: A switch that can vary the intensity of the light source that it controls.

Door casing: The trim applied to a wall around the edge of a door frame.

Double-glazed window: A window consisting of two panes of glass separated by a space that contains air or argon gas. The space provides most of the insulation.

Double-hung window: A window that consists of two framed-glass panels that slide open vertically, guided by a metal or wood track.

Downlighting: A lighting technique that illuminates objects or areas from above.

Duct: A tube or passage for venting indoor air to the outside.

Enclosure: Any material used to form a shower or tub stall, such as glass, glass block, or a tile wall.

Escutcheon: A decorative plate that covers a hole in the wall in which the pipe stem or cartridge fits.

Faux painting: Various painting techniques that mimic wood, marble, and other stones.

Fittings: The plumbing devices that transport water to the fixtures. These can include showerheads, faucets, and spouts. Also pertains to hardware and some accessories, such as towel racks, soap dishes, and toilet-paper dispensers.

Fixed window: A window that cannot be opened. It is usually a decorative unit, such as a half-round or Palladian-style window.

Fixture: Any fixed part of the structural design, such as tubs, bidets, toilets, and lavatories.

Fixture spacing: The amount of space included between ambient light fixtures to achieve an even field of illumination in a given area.

Fluorescent lamp: An energy-efficient light source made of a tube with an interior phosphorus coating that glows when energized by electricity.

Flux: The material applied to the surface of copper pipes and fittings when soldering to assist in the cleaning and bonding process.

Foot-candle (Fc): A unit that is used to measure the brightness produced by a lamp. A foot-candle is equal to one lumen per square foot of surface.

Form: The shape and structure of space or an object.

Full bath: A bath that includes a toilet, lavatory, and bathing fixture, such as a tub or shower.

Furring: Wood strips used to level parts of a ceiling, wall, or floor before adding the finish surface. Also used to secure panels of rigid insulation. Sometimes called strapping.

Glass blocks: Decorative building blocks made of translucent glass used for non-load-bearing walls to allow passage of light.

Glazing (walls): A technique for applying a thinned, tinted wash of translucent color to a dry undercoat of paint.

Ground-fault circuit interrupter (GFCI): A safety circuit breaker that compares the amount of current entering a receptacle with the amount leaving. If there is a discrepancy of 0.005 volt, the GFCI breaks the circuit in a fraction of a second. GFCIs are required by the National Electrical Code in areas of the house that are subject to dampness.

Grout: A binder and filler applied in the joints between ceramic tile.

Half bath (powder room): A bathroom that contains only a toilet and a sink.

Halogen bulb: A bulb filled with halogen gas, a substance that causes the particles of tungsten to be redeposited onto the tungsten filament. This process extends the lamp's life and makes the light whiter and brighter.

Hardboard: Manufactured pressed-wood panels; hardboard is rejected by some manufacturers as an acceptable substrate for resilient and tile floors.

Highlight: The lightest tone in a room.

Incandescent lamp: A bulb that contains a conductive filament through which current flows. The current reacts with an inert gas inside the bulb, which makes the filament glow.

Intensity: Strength of a color.

Jamb: The frame around a window or door.

Jets: Nozzles installed behind the walls of tubs or showers that pump out pressurized streams of water.

Joist: Set in a parallel fashion, these framing members support the boards of a ceiling or a floor.

Junction box: Electrical box in which all standard wiring splices and connections are made.

Lavatory or lav: A fixed bowl or basin with running water and a drainpipe that is used for washing.

Load-bearing wall: A wall that supports a structure's vertical load. Openings in any load-bearing wall must be reinforced to carry the live and dead weight of the structure's load.

Low-voltage lights: Lights that operate on 12 to 50 volts rather than the standard 120 volts.

Lumen: A term that refers to the intensity of light measured at a light source that is used for general or ambient lighting.

Medallion: A decorative, usually round relief, carving applied to a wall.

Molding: Decorative strips of wood or plastic used in various kinds of trimwork.

Muntins: Framing members of a window that divide the panes of glass.

Nonbearing wall: A wall that does not support the weight of areas above it.

On center: A point of reference for measuring. For example, 16 inches on center means 16 inches from the center of one framing member to the center of the next.

Overflow: An outlet positioned in a tub or sink that allows water to escape if a faucet is left open.

Palette: A range of colors that complement each other.

Pedestal: A stand-alone lavatory with a basin and supporting column in one piece.

Pilaster: A vertical relief molding attached to a wall, usually made to resemble the surface of a pillar.

Pocket door: A door that opens by sliding inside the wall, as opposed to a conventional door that opens into a room.

Pressure-balancing valve: Also known as a surge protector or antiscalding device. It is a control that prevents surges of hot or cold water in faucets by equalizing the amounts of hot and cold water pumped out at any time.

Proportion: The relationship of one object to another.

Radiant floor heat: A type of heating that is brought into a room via electrical wire or pipes (to carry hot water) that have been installed under the floor. As the pipes or electrical wire heats up, the flooring material warms and heat rises into the room.

Ragging: A painting technique that uses a crumpled piece of cloth to apply or remove small amounts of wet paint to create a pattern or texture.

Rail: Horizontal trimwork installed on a wall between the cornice and base trim. It may stand alone, as a chair rail, or be part of a larger framework.

Reflectance levels: The amount of light that is reflected from a colored surface, such as a tile wall or painted surface.

Resilient flooring: Thin floor coverings composed of materials such as vinyl, rubber, cork, or linoleum. Comes in a wide range of colors and patterns in both tile and sheet forms.

Rigid foam: Insulating boards composed of polystyrene or polyisocyanurate that may be foil backed. Rigid insulation offers the highest R-value per inch of thickness.

Roof window: A horizontal window that is installed on the roof. Roof windows are ventilating.

Roughing-in: The installation of the water-supply and DWV pipes before the fixtures are in place.

Rubber float: A flat, rubber-faced tool used to apply grout.

Scale: The size of a room or object.

Schematic: A detailed diagram of systems within a home.

Sconce: A decorative wall bracket, sometimes made of iron or glass, which shields a bulb.

Sight line: The natural line of sight the eye travels along when looking into or around a room.

Sister joist: A reinforcing joist added to the side of a cut or damaged joist for additional support.

Skylight: A framed opening in the roof that admits sunlight into the house. It can be covered with either a flat glass panel or a plastic dome.

Sliding window: Similar to a double-hung window turned on its side. The glass panels slide horizontally.

Snap-in grilles: Ready-made rectangular and diamond-pattern grilles that snap into a window sash and create the look of a true divided-light window.

Soffit: A boxed-in area just below the ceiling and above the vanity.

Soil stack: The main vertical pipe in a house that carries waste to the sewer or septic lines.

Spa: An inground or aboveground tublike structure or vessel that is equipped with whirlpool jets.

Space reconfiguration: A design term that is used to describe the reallocation of interior space without adding on.

Sponging: A paint technique that uses a small sponge to apply or remove small amounts of wet paint to create a pattern or texture on a surface.

Spout: The tube or pipe from which water gushes out of a faucet.

Spud washer: The large rubber ring placed over the drain hole of a two-piece toilet. The tank is placed over the spud washer.

Stencil: A design cut out of plastic or cardboard. When paint is applied to the cutout area, the design will be reproduced on a surface.

Stippling: A decorative paint technique that involves applying paint to a wall with a stiff bristle brush.

Stock cabinets: Cabinets that are in stock or available quickly when ordered from a retail outlet.

Stops: On doors, the trim on the jamb that keeps the door from swinging through; on windows, the trim that covers the inside face of the jamb.

Stud: The vertical member of a frame wall placed at both ends and usually every 16 inches on center.

A stud provides structural framing and facilitates covering with drywall or plywood.

Subfloor: The flooring applied directly to the floor joists on top of which the finished floor rests.

Surround: The enclosure and area around a tub or shower. A surround may include steps and a platform, as well as the tub itself.

Switch loop: Installation in which a switch is at the end of a circuit with one incoming power cable, and the outgoing neutral wire becomes a hot wire to control a fixture.

Task lighting: Lighting designed to illuminate a particular task, such as shaving.

Thickset: A layer of mortar that is more than ½ inch thick and is used as a base for setting ceramic tile.

Thinset: Any cement-based or organic adhesive applied in a layer less than ½ inch thick that is used for setting tile.

Three-quarter bath: A bathroom that contains a toilet, sink, and shower.

Tone: The degree of lightness or darkness of a color.

Tongue-and-groove: Boards milled with a protruding tongue on one edge and a slot on the other for a tight fit on flooring and paneling.

Traditional style: A style of decoration or architecture (typically of the eighteenth and nineteenth centuries) that employs forms that have been repeated for generations without major changes.

Trap: A section of curved pipe that forms a seal against sewer gas when it is filled with water.

Tripwaste: A lever-controlled bathtub drain stopper.

Trompe l'oeil: French for "fool the eye." A paint technique that creates a photographically real illusion of space or objects.

True divided-light window: A window composed of multiple glass panes that are divided by and held together by muntins.

Universal design: Products and designs that are easy to use by people of all ages, heights, and varying physical abilities.

Vanity: The countertop and cabinet unit that supports a sink. The vanity is usually included in the bathroom for storage purposes. It may also be used as a dressing table.

Vapor retarder: A material used to prevent water vapor from moving from one area into another or into a building material.

Vent stack: The main vertical vent pipe in the DWV system.

Ventilation: The process of removing or supplying air to a certain space.

Watt: The unit of measurement of electrical power required or consumed by a fixture or appliance.

Wax ring: A wax seal between the base of a toilet and the closet flange that prevents leaking.

Whirlpool: A special tub that includes motorized jets behind the walls of the tub for water massages.

Window stool: The horizontal surface installed below the sash of a window, often called a windowsill.

Wire connector: A small cap used for twisting two or more wires together.

Xenon bulb: A bulb similar to a halogen bulb, except that it is filled with xenon gas and does not emit ultraviolet (UV) rays. In addition, it is cooler and more energy efficient.

index

photo credits

pages 1–2: davidduncanlivingston.com **page 5:** Stacy Bass **page 7:** Eric Roth, design: fbnconstruction.net **pages 8–9:** Mark Samu, design/architect: Andrea Letkovsky AIA **pages 10–11:** *left* Mark Lohman, design: Malibu Interiors & Design; *right* Eric Roth, design: heidipribell.com **pages 12–13:** Eric Roth **pages 14–15:** *top left* courtesy of Neptune; *bottom left & right* Mark Lohman **pages 16–17:** *all* Mark Lohman, design: William Hefner Inc. **pages 18–19:** *left* Bob Greenspan, stylist: Susan Andrews; *all others* courtesy of Kohler **pages 20–21:** *all* Bob Greenspan, stylist: Susan Andrews **pages 22–23:** *top middle* Johnny Bouchier/Red Cover; *bottom left* Eric Roth, design: fbnconstruction.net; *bottom right* courtesy of Wetstyle **pages 24–25:** Julian Wass, design: Hein + Cozzi Inc. **pages 26–27:** *all* Mark Lohman **page 28:** Mark Lohman, design: Kathryne Designs **pages 30–31:** *all* Mark Samu, design/architect: Andrea Letkovsky AIA **pages 32–33:** *all* Eric Roth, design: bkarch.com **pages 34–35:** Olson Photographic, LLC, design/builder: Timberdale Homes **pages 36–37:** *all* davidduncanlivingston.com **pages 38–39:** *top left* davidduncanlivingston.com; *bottom middle* Bob Greenspan, stylist: Susan Andrews; *bottom right* Eric Roth, design: svdesign.com **pages 40–41:** *both* davidduncanlivingston.com **page 43:** Eric Roth, design: trikeenan.com **page 44:** *left* Olson Photographic, LLC, architect: Bartels Pagliaro Architects; *right* Joseph De Leo **page 45:** *left* Eric Roth, design: zeroenergy.com; *right* Mark Lohman, design: Janet Lohman Interior Design **page 46:** Julian

Wass, design: Angie Hranowski Design Studio **page 47:** Eric Roth, design: christinetuttle.com **page 49:** *all* Anne Gummerson, design: kitchensbyrequest.com **page 51:** *all* Karyn Millet/Red Cover, design: The Warwick Group **pages 52–53:** *all* Bob Greenspan, stylist: Susan Andrews **page 54:** Eric Roth, design: heidipribell.com **pages 56–57:** *all* Mark Samu, design: Evergreen Interiors **page 58:** *both* davidduncanlivingston.com **page 60:** *left* Eric Roth, design: John DeBastiani; *right* Olson Photographic, LLC, design: Capitol designs **page 61:** *left* Olson Photographic, LLC, design: Design Build; *top & bottom right* Eric Roth, (*bottom* design: John DeBastiani) **pages 62–63:** *all* Mark Samu (*left both* architect: Robert Storm AIA) **pages 64–65:** Bob Greenspan, stylist: Susan Andrews **pages 66–67:** *both* Eric Roth, design: ruhlwalker.com **page 68:** *top* courtesy of Neptune; *bottom* courtesy of Caroma **page 69:** *left* Bob Greenspan, stylist: Susan Andrews; *top right* courtesy of Stone Forest; *middle right* courtesy of JACLO; *bottom right* courtesy of Moen **page 70:** *top* Bob Greenspan, stylist: Susan Andrews; *bottom* courtesy of Hastings Tile & Bath **page 71:** *top* courtesy of Stone Forest; *bottom* courtesy of Laufen **pages 72–73:** *all* Olson Photographic, LLC, design: Stacey Gendelman Designs **pages 74–75:** *all* Jerry Pavia **page 76:** Karyn Millet/Red Cover, design: Molly Isaksen **page 77:** *top & bottom left* Eric Roth, (*bottom* design: morseconstructions.com); *right* davidduncanlivingston.com **pages 78–79:** *all* davidduncanlivingston.com **pages 80–81:** *all* Mark Lohman, design: Janet

Lohman Interior Design **pages 82–83:** *left all* courtesy of JACLO; *center both* Mark Samu, design: Suzette O'Farrell Design; *right* courtesy of MGSProgetti.com **page 84:** Stacy Bass **page 85:** *top left* courtesy of Stone Forest; *top right* Mark Lohman; *bottom right* Eric Roth, design: jwconstruction-inc.com; *bottom left* davidduncanlivingston.com **page 86:** *both* Stacy Bass **page 87:** Eric Roth **page 88:** *top left & bottom right* Bob Greenspan, stylist: Susan Andrews; *bottom left* courtesy of Hastings Tile & Bath **page 89:** *top left* Bob Greenspan, stylist: Susan Andrews; *top right both* Mark Samu, design: Really at Home; *bottom left* courtesy of Moen **page 90:** *top* courtesy of Kohler; *bottom right* courtesy of Caroma; *bottom left both* Mark Samu, design: Really at Home **page 91:** courtesy of Toto **pages 92–93:** *bottom left, top left center & top right* courtesy of Neo-Metro; *top right center* courtesy of Herbeau; *bottom center & right all* courtesy of Moen **pages 94–95:** Mark Samu, design: Bonacio Construction **pages 96–97:** *left* Mark Lohman, design: Janet Lohman Interior Design; *center* Stacy Bass; *top right* Tony Giammarino/Giammarino & Dworkin, design/architect: evolvearchitecture.com; *bottom right* courtesy of REHAU **page 98:** *left* Tony Giammarino/Giammarino & Dworkin, design/architect: evolvearchitecture.com; *top right* Mark Samu, design: Bonacio Construction; *bottom right* davidduncanlivingston.com **page 99:** davidduncanlivingston.com **pages 100–101:** *both* Eric Roth, design: christofiinteriors.com **pages 102–103:** *both* Eric Roth **pages 104–105:** *all* Tony Giammarino/Giammarino & Dworkin, design/architect: evolvearchitecture.com **page 106:** *left* Mark Samu, design: Jeanne Ziering Design; *right* davidduncanlivingston.com **page 107:** Mark Lohman, design: Lynn Pries Design **page 108:** davidduncanlivingston.com **page 109:** *left* Grant Govier/Red Cover; *right* Paul Ryan-Goff/Red Cover **pages 110–111:** *both* Eric Roth, *left* design: mtruant.com, *right* design: trikeenan.com **page 112:** courtesy of Caesarstone **page 113:** Bob Greenspan, stylist: Susan Andrews, design: Elizabeth Goltz, designbyorion.com **page 114:** *top* Tony Giammarino/Giammarino & Dworkin, design: homemasons.com; *bottom* courtesy of Corian **page 115:** *both* davidduncanlivingston.com **page 116:** *left* Eric Roth; *right* davidduncanlivingston.com **page 117:** *left* Tony Giammarino/Giammarino & Dworkin, design: SandraVitzthum.com; *right* Eric Roth, design: Planeta Basque Boston LLC **pages 118–119:** *all* Mark Samu, design: Jeanne Ziering Design **pages 120–121:** Bob Greenspan, stylist: Susan Andrews **page 122:** Eric Roth, design: daherinteriordesign.com **page 123:** *left* Eric Roth, design: GFCDevelopment.com; *right* Stacy Bass **pages 124–125:** *both* Mark Lohman, design: Taddey & Karlin Design **pages 126–127:** *all* Eric Roth, *left* design: baypointbuilderscorp.com, *center* design: Planeta Basque Boston LLC, *right* design/build: jwconstructioninc.com **page 128:** courtesy of Merillat **page 129:** Olson Photography, LLC, architect: Peter Cadoux Architects **pages 130–131:** *all* courtesy of Merillat **page 132:** davidduncanlivingston.com **page 133:** Eric Roth **page 134:** courtesy of Merillat **page 135:** davidduncanlivingston.com **page 136:** *top* Eric Roth, design/build: howelldesignbuild.com; *bottom* courtesy of

Kohler/Robern **page 137:** *both* Eric Roth, *top* design: Tricia McDonagh Interior Design, *bottom* design/architect: Hickox Williams **pages 138–139:** *all* Tony Giammarino/Giammarino & Dworkin, design: LeslieStephensDesign.net **page 140:** *top left* Mark Lohman, design: Janet Lohman Interior Design; *top right & bottom left* davidduncanlivingston.com; *bottom right* courtesy of Kraftmaid **page 141:** courtesy of Wood-Mode **pages 142–143:** *left & both middle* courtesy of Merillat; *right* courtesy of Kraftmaid **page 144:** *top* Mark Lohman; *bottom* Tony Giammarino/Giammarino & Dworkin, design/architect: evolvearchitecture.com **page 145:** Eric Roth, design: hutkerarchitects.com **pages 146–147:** Mark Lohman, design: GSGibson Inc. **page 148:** Anne Gummerson, design: Rhea Arnot Design **pages 149–151:** davidduncanlivingston.com **page 152:** *both* Eric Roth, *left* design: svdesign.com; *right* design/build: morseconstructions.com **page 153:** Mark Lohman, architect: Michael Lee Architects **page 154:** *left* Eric Roth; *right* Mark Samu **page 155:** davidduncanlivingston.com **pages 156–157:** *all* melabee m miller, design: Tammy Kaplan **page 158:** *left* davidduncanlivingston.com; *right* Eric Roth, design: sternmccafferty.com **page 159:** Mark Lohman, design: GSGibson Inc. **pages 160–161:** Olson Photographic, LLC, design/build: Hobbs, Inc. **page 162:** *left* Eric Roth, design: paynebouchier.com; *right* davidduncanlivingston.com **page 163:** Eric Roth, design/architect: spacecraftarch.com **page 164:** *both* Olson Photographic, LLC, *left* design/build: Hobbs, Inc., *right* design/build: Coastal Point Development **page 165:** *both* Mark Samu, *left* architect: Ellen Roche AIA, *right* design/build: Bonacio Construc-

tion **page 166:** *left* melabee m miller, design: Nancee Brown, ASID; *right* davidduncanlivingston.com **page 167:** Tony Giammarino/Giammarino & Dworkin, design/architect: evolvearchitecture.com **page 168:** *both* Mark Lohman, *top* design: Taddey & Karlin Design **page 169:** Mark Lohman **pages 170–171:** melabee m miller, design: Nancee Brown, ASID **page 172:** *top* davidduncanlivingston.com; *bottom* Mark Lohman, design: Harte Brownlee & Assoc. **page 173:** Olson Photographic, LLC, design/build: Country Club Homes **pages 174–175:** Eric Roth, design: whitlabrothers.com **pages 176–177:** davidduncanlivingston.com **page 178:** Mark Lohman, design: Barclay Butera Inc. **page 179:** Olson Photographic, LLC **pages 180–181:** *both* davidduncanlivingston.com **pages 182–183:** Eric Roth, design: traskdevelopment.com **pages 184–185:** Olson Photographic, LLC, design/build: Ricci Construction **pages 186–187:** Eric Roth, design: Elisa Allen Interiors **pages 188–189:** *all* Mark Lohman **pages 190–191:** davidduncanlivingston.com **pages 192–193:** *all* Mark Lohman, architect: Michael Lee Architects **page 194:** *left* Bob Greenspan, stylist: Susan Andrews; *right* Mark Lohman **pages 195–197:** davidduncanlivingston.com **pages 198–199:** *both* Bob Greenspan, stylist: Susan Andrews **pages 200–201:** *all* Mark Lohman, design: Malibu Interiors & Design **page 202:** *both* melabee m miller, design: Nancee Brown, ASID **page 203:** melabee m miller, design: Diane Romanowski **page 211:** davidduncanlivingston.com **page 212:** Anne Gummerson, design: Rhea Arnot Design **page 215:** Mark Lohman, design: Taddey & Karlin Design **page 218:** Stacy Bass **page 221:** davidduncanlivingston.com

Have a gardening, decorating, or home improvement project?
Look for these and other fine Creative Homeowner books wherever books are sold

BEST SIGNATURE KITCHENS

A showcase of kitchens from top designers around the country.

Over 250 photographs.
240 pp.
8¼" × 10⅞"
$19.95 (US)
$23.95 (CAN)
BOOK #: CH279510

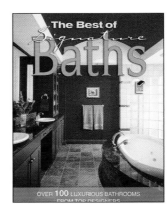

THE BEST OF SIGNATURE BATHS

Features luxurious and inspiring bathrooms from top designers.

Over 250 photographs.
240 pp.
8¼" × 10⅞"
$19.95 (US)
$21.95 (CAN)
BOOK #: CH279522

CAN'T FAIL COLOR SCHEMES

A take-it-with you visual guide to selecting color schemes and texture.

Over 300 photographs.
304 pp.
7" × 9¼"
$19.95 (US)
$21.95 (CAN)
BOOK #: CH279659

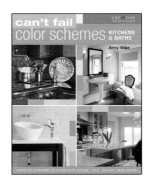

CAN'T FAIL COLOR SCHEMES—KITCHENS & BATHS

A guide to color ideas for kitchens and baths.

Over 300 photographs.
304 pp.
7" × 9¼"
$19.95 (US)
$21.95 (CAN)
BOOK #: CH279648

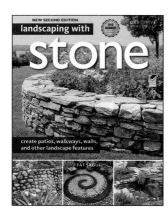

LANDSCAPING WITH STONE

Ideas for incorporating stone into the landscape.

Over 335 photographs.
224 pp.
8½" × 10⅞"
$19.95 (US)
$21.95 (CAN)
BOOK #: CH274179

SUCCESSFUL CONTAINER GARDENING

Information to grow your own flower, fruit, and vegetable "gardens."

Over 240 photographs.
160 pp.
8½" × 10⅞"
$14.95 (US)
$17.95 (CAN)
BOOK #: CH274857